Tail
children's

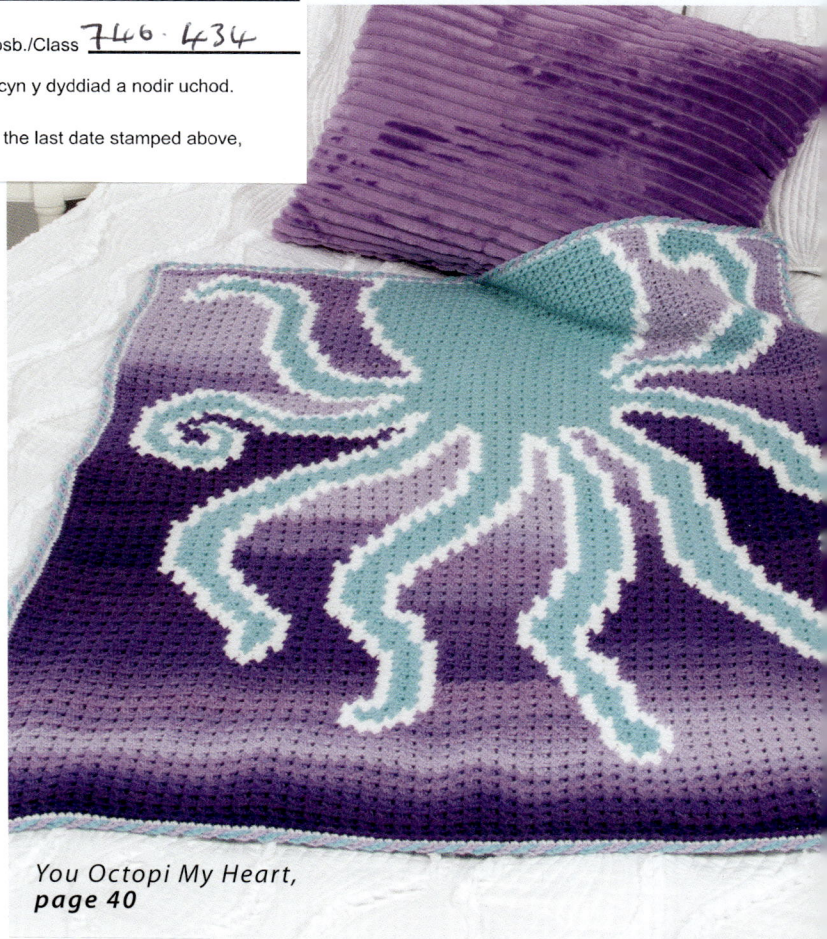

Shark Bait,
page 31

You Octopi My Heart,
page 40

Table of Contents

General Instructions

Pattern & Color Chart Instructions

The pattern is provided in two formats: detailed written instructions and a color chart with matching color key. Use the format you prefer.

The written instructions specify the yarn color and stitch count. Read all instructions to assist with comprehension of the written format. Detailed written instructions and a symbol diagram are included for the border of the blanket.

If following the color chart, a foundation row of 122 single crochet must be completed before chart instructions begin.

The chart is worked with 60 stitches per row and a total of 125 rows (not counting the foundation row)

Each square on the chart instructions represents one mini V-stitch (see figure below; red mini V-stitch represents 1 square).

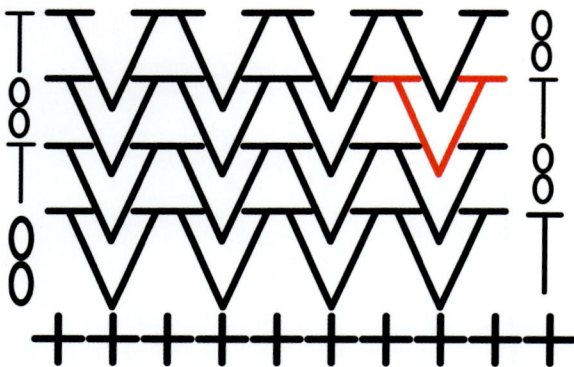

Each row will begin with a chain-2 and end with a half double crochet in top of the beginning chain of the prior row, these stitches are not shown on the color chart.

When working from the color chart, row 1 will begin with a chain-2, skip one stitch, [mini V-stitch in next stitch, skip next stitch], repeat between [ ] across the row, ending with a half double crochet in the last stitch and turn (refer to above chart).

For all remaining rows, begin with a chain-2, work each mini V-stitch **between** the half double crochets of the mini V-stitch of the prior row (do not work in the top of the stitch). At the end of each row work a half double crochet in the top of the beginning chain of the previous row.

The placement of the mini V-stitch is in the **space** between half double crochets of the prior row's mini V-stitches, not in top of the half double crochets. *(See Photo 1)*

Photo 1

Color Change Instructions

When pattern (written or color chart) indicates to change yarn color, change yarn in last step of prior stitch.

When working mini V-stitch, work the first half double crochet in main color (MC). *(See Photo 2)*

Photo 2

For second half double crochet, yarn over, insert hook, pull up a loop, drop MC, yarn over with contrasting color (CC) *(See Photo 3)*,

Photo 3

pull through all 3 loops on hook. *(See Photo 4)*

Photo 4

Complete the next mini V-stitch in the CC. *(See Photo 5)*

Photo 5

How to Hide Yarn When Carrying Color Up to Next Row

When CC is being used in the corresponding stitches of the next row in the pattern, use the dropped yarn from prior row to continue with the CC. If the stitches do not line up exactly (color changes in squares on chart are not directly on top of one another), you will be able to see the yarn being carried up. You will want to bury this yarn in the next mini V-stitches. *(See Photo 6 and 7)*

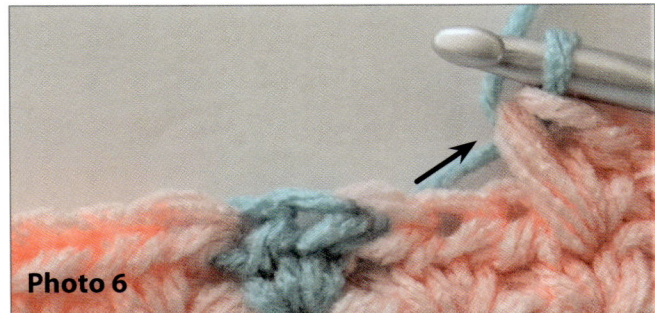

Photo 6

Front of work (showing yarn to hide)

Photo 7

Back of work (showing yarn to hide)

After changing yarn color in last step of prior mini V-stitch (shown in photos above), hide the piece of yarn by crocheting over it with the next mini V-stitch. *(See Photo 8, 9 and 10)*

Photo 8

Front of work (hiding yarn in next mini V-stitch)

Photo 9

Front of work (mini V-stitch completed)

Photo 10

Back of work (still showing some yarn)

To hide the small section of yarn still showing after first mini V-stitch has been completed, begin next mini V-stitch by yarning over and inserting hook in completed stitch. At this point, rotate your hook in the direction of the yarn you want to hide. Grab this piece of yarn *(see where hook placement is in photo 11)*,

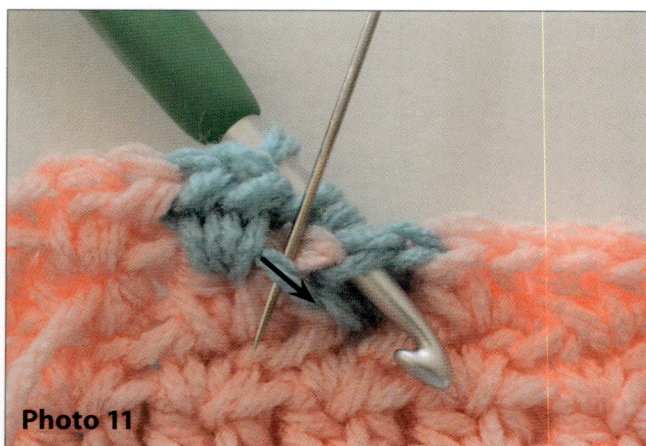

Photo 11

Back of work (yarn to hide)

then complete the half double crochet and next half double crochet to complete the mini V-stitch. *(See Photo 12 and 13)*

Photo 12

Back of work (complete mini V-stitch)

Photo 13

Back of work (where yarn is hidden)

The yarn being carried up is now hidden, giving your crochet piece a clean appearance.

Twisting Border

Note: Black dot in each photo indicates next st placement.

Rnd 1: Join MC with sl st in top of first sc of row 1, ch 4, sk next 3 sts, sl st in next st *(See Photo 14)*,

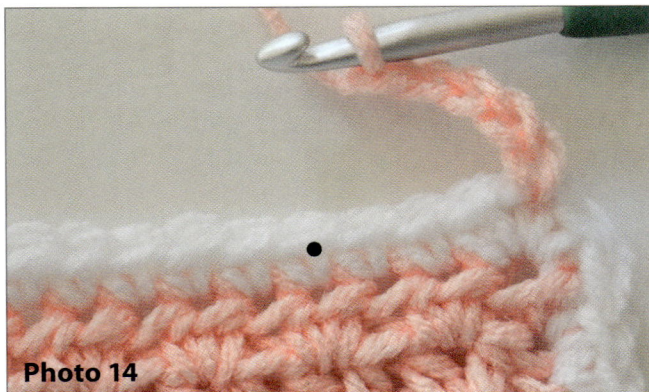

Photo 14

extend lp on hook and remove hook from yarn *(See Photo 15)*,

Photo 15

push ch lp just made to front of blanket, *working behind ch lp made, join CC with sl st in 2nd sk st between ch lp *(See Photo 16)*,

Photo 16

ch 4, sk next 3 sts (including st with MC sl st), sl st in next st *(See Photo 17)*,

Photo 17

extend lp on hook and remove hook from yarn, push new ch lp just made to front of blanket, working behind ch lp just made, pull extended lp of MC to back of blanket *(See Photo 18)*,

Photo 18

pull lp tight on hook, ch 4, sk next 3 sts (including st with CC sl st), sl st in next st *(See Photo 19)*,

Photo 19

extend lp on hook and remove hook from yarn, hold new ch lp just made to front of blanket (See Photo 20),

Photo 20

Photo 21

rep from * around entire blanket until each color meets first st it was worked in. (See Photo 21)

Fasten off each color. ●

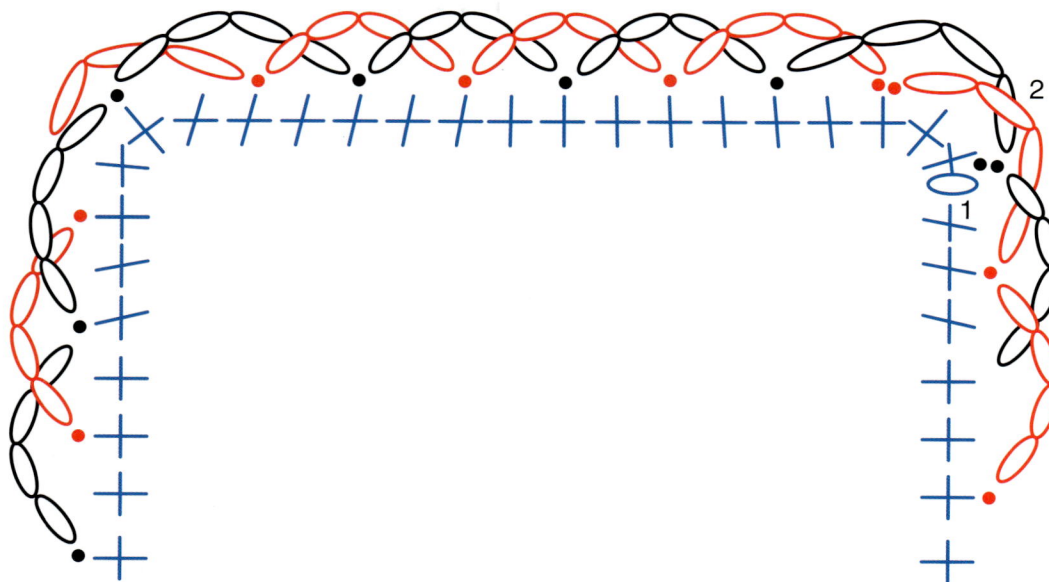

Twisting Border
Reduced Sample of Stitch Diagram

STITCH KEY	
⬭	Chain (ch)
•	Slip stitch (sl st)
+	Single crochet (sc)

Mermaid Dreams

Skill Level

■■■□□ EASY

Finished Measurements

Approximately 38 inches wide x 48 inches long

Materials

- Red Heart Super Saver medium (worsted) weight acrylic yarn (7 oz/364 yds/198g per skein):
  4 skeins #774 light raspberry (MC)
  1 skein #311 white (CC2)
- Red Heart Super Saver Ombré medium (worsted) weight acrylic yarn (10 oz/ 482 yds/283g per skein):
  1 skein #3985 deep teal (CC)
- Size I/9/5.5mm crochet hook or size needed to obtain gauge
- Tapestry needle
- Bobbins (optional)

4 MEDIUM

Gauge

11 sts = 4 inches; 15 rows = 4 inches

Pattern Notes

Before beginning, we suggest you read the General Instructions on pages 2–6 for information needed to work the pattern.

Refer to Stitch Diagrams and Color Chart as needed.

All rows begin with MC.

Weave in loose ends as work progresses.

Chain-2 at beginning of row counts as a half double crochet unless otherwise stated.

Special Stitch

Mini V-stitch (mini V-st): 2 hdc in indicated st or sp.

Afghan

Foundation row (WS): With MC, ch 123, sc in 2nd ch from hook and in each rem sc across, turn. *(122 sts)*

Row 1 (RS): Ch 2 *(see Pattern Notes)*, ***mini V-st** *(see Special Stitch)* in next st, sk next st, rep from * across to last st, hdc in last st, turn. *(60 sts, 2 hdc)*

Row 2: Ch 2, *mini V-st in between hdc of each mini V-st across, hdc in top of beg ch-2, turn.

Rows 3–8: Rep row 2.

Row 9: Ch 2, mini V-st in each of next 46 sts, **changing color** *(see General Instructions)* to CC2 in last leg of last mini V-st, mini V-st between hdc of each of next 2 mini V-sts, changing color to MC in last leg of last mini V-st, mini V-st between hdc of each of next 12 mini V-sts, hdc in top of beg ch-2, turn.

Note: On following rows, mini V-sts will be referred to as sts.

Row 10: Ch 2, work 10 sts, with CC2 work 6 sts, with MC work 44 sts, hdc in top of beg ch-2, turn.

Row 11: Ch 2, work 13 sts, with CC2 work 3 sts, with MC work 25 sts, with CC2 work 4 sts, with CC work 3 sts, with CC2 work 3 sts, with MC work 9 sts, hdc in top of beg ch-2, turn.

Row 12: Ch 2, work 8 sts, with CC2 work 2 sts, with CC work 8 sts, with CC2 work 3 sts, with MC work 21 sts, with CC2 work 6 sts, with MC work 12 sts, hdc in top of beg ch-2, turn.

Row 13: Ch 2, work 11 sts, with CC2 work 2 sts, with CC work 4 sts, with CC2 work 3 sts, with MC work 17 sts, with CC2 work 3 sts, with CC work 10 sts, with CC2 work 2 sts, with MC work 8 sts, hdc in top of beg ch-2, turn.

Row 14: Ch 2, work 9 sts, with CC2 work 1 st, with CC work 12 sts, with CC2 work 2 sts, with MC work 14 sts,

with CC2 work 3 sts, with CC work 7 sts, with CC2 work 2 sts, with MC work 10 sts, hdc in top of beg ch-2, turn.

Row 15: Ch 2, work 10 sts, with CC2 work 1 st, with CC work 10 sts, with CC2 work 3 sts, with MC work 11 sts, with CC2 work 2 sts, with CC work 12 sts, with CC2 work 2 sts, with MC work 9 sts, hdc in top of beg ch-2, turn.

Row 16: Ch 2, work 10 sts, with CC2 work 2 sts, with CC work 12 sts, with CC2 work 2 sts, with MC work 9 sts, with CC2 work 2 sts, with CC work 13 sts, with CC2 work 1 st, with MC work 9 sts, hdc in top of beg ch-2, turn.

Row 17: Ch 2, work 9 sts, with CC2 work 2 sts, with CC work 13 sts, with CC2 work 1 st, with MC work 8 sts, with CC2 work 2 sts, with CC work 13 sts, with CC2 work 1 st, with MC work 11 sts, hdc in top of beg ch-2, turn.

Row 18: Ch 2, work 11 sts, with CC2 work 2 sts, with CC work 13 sts, with CC2 work 1 st, with MC work 7 sts, with CC2 work 2 sts, with CC work 12 sts, with CC2 work 2 sts, with MC work 10 sts, hdc in top of beg ch-2, turn.

Row 19: Ch 2, work 11 sts, with CC2 work 2 sts, with CC work 12 sts, with CC2 work 1 st, with MC work 6 sts, with CC2 work 2 sts, with CC work 13 sts, with CC2 work 1 st, with MC work 12 sts, hdc in top of beg ch-2, turn.

Row 20: Ch 2, work 12 sts, with CC2 work 2 sts, with CC work 13 sts, with CC2 work 2 sts, with MC work 4 sts, with CC2 work 1 st, with CC work 13 sts, with CC2 work 1 st, with MC work 12 sts, hdc in top of beg ch-2, turn.

Row 21: Ch 2, work 12 sts, with CC2 work 2 sts, with CC work 12 sts, with CC2 work 1 st, with MC work 4 sts, with CC2 work 1 st, with CC work 14 sts, with CC2 work 1 st, with MC work 13 sts, hdc in top of beg ch-2, turn.

Row 22: Ch 2, work 13 sts, with CC2 work 2 sts, with CC work 13 sts, with CC2 work 1 st, with MC work 2 sts, with CC2 work 2 sts, with CC work 13 sts, with CC2 work 1 st, with MC work 13 sts, hdc in top of beg ch-2, turn.

Row 23: Ch 2, work 13 sts, with CC2 work 2 sts, with CC work 13 sts, with CC2 work 1 st, with MC work 1 st, with CC2 work 2 sts, with CC work 13 sts, with CC2 work 1 st, with MC work 14 sts, hdc in top of beg ch-2, turn.

Row 24: Ch 2, work 14 sts, with CC2 work 1 st, with CC work 14 sts, with CC2 work 3 sts, with CC work 12 sts, with CC2 work 2 sts, with MC work 14 sts, hdc in top of beg ch-2, turn.

Row 25: Ch 2, work 15 sts, with CC2 work 1 st, with CC work 13 sts, with CC2 work 2 sts, with CC work 13 sts, with CC2 work 2 sts, with MC work 14 sts, hdc in top of beg ch-2, turn.

Row 26: Ch 2, work 15 sts, with CC2 work 1 st, with CC work 27 sts, with CC2 work 2 sts, with MC work 15 sts, hdc in top of beg ch-2, turn.

Row 27: Ch 2, work 16 sts, with CC2 work 2 sts, with CC work 25 sts, with CC2 work 2 sts, with MC work 15 sts, hdc in top of beg ch-2, turn.

Row 28: Ch 2, work 16 sts, with CC2 work 1 st, with CC work 24 sts, with CC2 work 2 sts, with MC work 17 sts, hdc in top of beg ch-2, turn.

Row 29: Ch 2, work 18 sts, with CC2 work 2 sts, with CC work 22 sts, with CC2 work 2 sts, with MC work 16 sts, hdc in top of beg ch-2, turn.

Row 30: Ch 2, work 17 sts, with CC2 work 2 sts, with CC work 20 sts, with CC2 work 2 sts, with MC work 19 sts, hdc in top of beg ch-2, turn.

Row 31: Ch 2, work 20 sts, with CC2 work 2 sts, with CC work 19 sts, with CC2 work 1 st, with MC work 18 sts, hdc in top of beg ch-2, turn.

Row 32: Ch 2, work 18 sts, with CC2 work 2 sts, with CC work 17 sts, with CC2 work 2 sts, with MC work 21 sts, hdc in top of beg ch-2, turn.

Row 33: Ch 2, work 22 sts, with CC2 work 2 sts, with CC work 15 sts, with CC2 work 2 sts, with MC work 19 sts, hdc in top of beg ch-2, turn.

Row 34: Ch 2, work 20 sts, with CC2 work 2 sts, with CC work 12 sts, with CC2 work 3 sts, with MC work 23 sts, hdc in top of beg ch-2, turn.

Row 35: Ch 2, work 25 sts, with CC2 work 2 sts, with CC work 9 sts, with CC2 work 3 sts, with MC work 21 sts, hdc in top of beg ch-2, turn.

Row 36: Ch 2, work 22 sts, with CC2 work 3 sts, with CC work 5 sts, with CC2 work 4 sts, with MC work 26 sts, hdc in top of beg ch-2, turn.

Row 37: Ch 2, work 28 sts, with CC2 work 3 sts, with CC work 3 sts, with CC2 work 2 sts, with MC work 24 sts, hdc in top of beg ch-2, turn.

Row 38: Ch 2, work 25 sts, with CC2 work 1 st, with CC work 3 sts, with CC2 work 1 st, with MC work 30 sts, hdc in top of beg ch-2, turn.

Row 39: Ch 2, work 30 sts, with CC2 work 1 st, with CC work 3 sts, with CC2 work 1 st, with MC work 25 sts, hdc in top of beg ch-2, turn.

Row 40: Ch 2, work 25 sts, with CC2 work 1 st, with CC work 3 sts, with CC2 work 1 st, with MC work 30 sts, hdc in top of beg ch-2, turn.

Row 41: Ch 2, work 30 sts, with CC2 work 2 sts, with CC work 2 sts, with CC2 work 2 sts, with MC work 24 sts, hdc in top of beg ch-2, turn.

Row 42: Ch 2, work 24 sts, with CC2 work 1 st, with CC work 2 sts, with CC2 work 2 sts, with MC work 31 sts, hdc in top of beg ch-2, turn.

Row 43: Ch 2, work 32 sts, with CC2 work 1 st, with CC work 2 sts, with CC2 work 2 sts, with MC work 23 sts, hdc in top of beg ch-2, turn.

Row 44: Ch 2, work 22 sts, with CC2 work 2 sts, with CC work 3 sts, with CC2 work 1 st, with MC work 32 sts, hdc in top of beg ch-2, turn.

Row 45: Ch 2, work 32 sts, with CC2 work 1 st, with CC work 4 sts, with CC2 work 1 st, with MC work 22 sts, hdc in top of beg ch-2, turn.

Row 46: Ch 2, work 21 sts, with CC2 work 2 sts, with CC work 3 sts, with CC2 work 2 sts, with MC work 32 sts, hdc in top of beg ch-2, turn.

Row 47: Ch 2, work 33 sts, with CC2 work 1 st, with CC work 4 sts, with CC2 work 1 st, with MC work 21 sts, hdc in top of beg ch-2, turn.

Row 48: Ch 2, work 21 sts, with CC2 work 1 st, with CC work 4 sts, with CC2 work 1 st, with MC work 33 sts, hdc in top of beg ch-2, turn.

Row 49: Ch 2, work 33 sts, with CC2 work 1 st, with CC work 4 sts, with CC2 work 2 sts, with MC work 20 sts, hdc in top of beg ch-2, turn.

Row 50: Ch 2, work 20 sts, with CC2 work 2 sts, with CC work 4 sts, with CC2 work 1 st, with MC work 33 sts, hdc in top of beg ch-2, turn.

Row 51: Ch 2, work 33 sts, with CC2 work 1 st, with CC work 5 sts, with CC2 work 2 sts, with MC work 19 sts, hdc in top of beg ch-2, turn.

Row 52: Ch 2, work 19 sts, with CC2 work 1 st, with CC work 6 sts, with CC2 work 1 st, with MC work 33 sts, hdc in top of beg ch-2, turn.

Row 53: Ch 2, work 33 sts, with CC2 work 1 st, with CC work 6 sts, with CC2 work 1 st, with MC work 19 sts, hdc in top of beg ch-2, turn.

Row 54: Ch 2, work 18 sts, with CC2 work 2 sts, with CC work 6 sts, with CC2 work 1 st, with MC work 33 sts, hdc in top of beg ch-2, turn.

Row 55: Ch 2, work 33 sts, with CC2 work 1 st, with CC work 6 sts, with CC2 work 2 sts, with MC work 18 sts, hdc in top of beg ch-2, turn.

Row 56: Ch 2, work 18 sts, with CC2 work 1 st, with CC work 7 sts, with CC2 work 1 st, with MC work 33 sts, hdc in top of beg ch-2, turn.

Row 57: Ch 2, work 33 sts, with CC2 work 1 st, with CC work 7 sts, with CC2 work 1 st, with MC work 18 sts, hdc in top of beg ch-2, turn.

Row 58: Ch 2, work 18 sts, with CC2 work 1 st, with CC work 7 sts, with CC2 work 2 sts, with MC work 32 sts, hdc in top of beg ch-2, turn.

Row 59: Ch 2, work 32 sts, with CC2 work 2 sts, with CC work 7 sts, with CC2 work 1 st, with MC work 18 sts, hdc in top of beg ch-2, turn.

Row 60: Ch 2, work 17 sts, with CC2 work 2 sts, with CC work 8 sts, with CC2 work 1 st, with MC work 32 sts, hdc in top of beg ch-2, turn.

Row 61: Ch 2, work 31 sts, with CC2 work 2 sts, with CC work 9 sts, with CC2 work 1 st, with MC work 17 sts, hdc in top of beg ch-2, turn.

Row 62: Ch 2, work 17 sts, with CC2 work 1 st, with CC work 9 sts, with CC2 work 2 sts, with MC work 31 sts, hdc in top of beg ch-2, turn.

Row 63: Ch 2, work 31 sts, with CC2 work 1 st, with CC work 10 sts, with CC2 work 1 st, with MC work 17 sts, hdc in top of beg ch-2, turn.

Row 64: Ch 2, work 17 sts, with CC2 work 1 st, with CC work 10 sts, with CC2 work 1 st, with MC work 31 sts, hdc in top of beg ch-2, turn.

Row 65: Ch 2, work 30 sts, with CC2 work 2 sts, with CC work 10 sts, with CC2 work 2 sts, with MC work 16 sts, hdc in top of beg ch-2, turn.

Row 66: Ch 2, work 16 sts, with CC2 work 2 sts, with CC work 11 sts, with CC2 work 2 sts, with MC work 29 sts, hdc in top of beg ch-2, turn.

Row 67: Ch 2, work 29 sts, with CC2 work 1 st, with CC work 12 sts, with CC2 work 2 sts, with MC work 16 sts, hdc in top of beg ch-2, turn.

Row 68: Ch 2, work 16 sts, with CC2 work 1 st, with CC work 13 sts, with CC2 work 2 sts, with MC work 28 sts, hdc in top of beg ch-2, turn.

Row 69: Ch 2, work 28 sts, with CC2 work 1 st, with CC work 14 sts, with CC2 work 1 st, with MC work 16 sts, hdc in top of beg ch-2, turn.

Row 70: Ch 2, work 16 sts, with CC2 work 1 st, with CC work 14 sts, with CC2 work 1 st, with MC work 28 sts, hdc in top of beg ch-2, turn.

Row 71: Ch 2, work 28 sts, with CC2 work 1 st, with CC work 14 sts, with CC2 work 1 st, with MC work 16 sts, hdc in top of beg ch-2, turn.

Row 72: Ch 2, work 16 sts, with CC2 work 1 st, with CC work 14 sts, with CC2 work 2 sts, with MC work 27 sts, hdc in top of beg ch-2, turn.

Row 73: Ch 2, work 27 sts, with CC2 work 1 st, with CC work 15 sts, with CC2 work 1 st, with MC work 16 sts, hdc in top of beg ch-2, turn.

Row 74: Ch 2, work 16 sts, with CC2 work 1 st, with CC work 15 sts, with CC2 work 2 sts, with MC work 26 sts, hdc in top of beg ch-2, turn.

Row 75: Ch 2, work 26 sts, with CC2 work 1 st, with CC work 16 sts, with CC2 work 1 st, with MC work 16 sts, hdc in top of beg ch-2, turn.

Row 76: Ch 2, work 16 sts, with CC2 work 2 sts, with CC work 15 sts, with CC2 work 1 st, with MC work 26 sts, hdc in top of beg ch-2, turn.

Row 77: Ch 2, work 25 sts, with CC2 work 2 sts, with CC work 15 sts, with CC2 work 2 sts, with MC work 16 sts, hdc in top of beg ch-2, turn.

Row 78: Ch 2, work 17 sts, with CC2 work 1 st, with CC work 16 sts, with CC2 work 1 st, with MC work 25 sts, hdc in top of beg ch-2, turn.

Row 79: Ch 2, work 24 sts, with CC2 work 2 sts, with CC work 15 sts, with CC2 work 2 sts, with MC work 17 sts, hdc in top of beg ch-2, turn.

Row 80: Ch 2, work 18 sts, with CC2 work 1 st, with CC work 15 sts, with CC2 work 2 sts, with MC work 24 sts, hdc in top of beg ch-2, turn.

Row 81: Ch 2, work 24 sts, with CC2 work 1 st, with CC work 16 sts, with CC2 work 1 st, with MC work 18 sts, hdc in top of beg ch-2, turn.

Row 82: Ch 2, work 18 sts, with CC2 work 1 st, with CC work 16 sts, with CC2 work 1 st, with MC work 24 sts, hdc in top of beg ch-2, turn.

Row 83: Ch 2, work 24 sts, with CC2 work 1 st, with CC work 15 sts, with CC2 work 2 sts, with MC work 18 sts, hdc in top of beg ch-2, turn.

Row 84: Ch 2, work 18 sts, with CC2 work 2 sts, with CC work 15 sts, with CC2 work 2 sts, with MC work 23 sts, hdc in top of beg ch-2, turn.

Row 85: Ch 2, work 23 sts, with CC2 work 2 sts, with CC work 15 sts, with CC2 work 1 st, with MC work 19 sts, hdc in top of beg ch-2, turn.

Row 86: Ch 2, work 19 sts, with CC2 work 1 st, with CC work 16 sts, with CC2 work 1 st, with MC work 23 sts, hdc in top of beg ch-2, turn.

Row 87: Ch 2, work 23 sts, with CC2 work 1 st, with CC work 15 sts, with CC2 work 2 sts, with MC work 19 sts, hdc in top of beg ch-2, turn.

Row 88: Ch 2, work 19 sts, with CC2 work 2 sts, with CC work 15 sts, with CC2 work 1 st, with MC work 23 sts, hdc in top of beg ch-2, turn.

Row 89: Ch 2, work 23 sts, with CC2 work 1 st, with CC work 15 sts, with CC2 work 1 st, with MC work 20 sts, hdc in top of beg ch-2, turn.

Row 90: Ch 2, work 20 sts, with CC2 work 1 st, with CC work 15 sts, with CC2 work 1 st, with MC work 23 sts, hdc in top of beg ch-2, turn.

Row 91: Ch 2, work 22 sts, with CC2 work 2 sts, with CC work 15 sts, with CC2 work 1 st, with MC work 20 sts, hdc in top of beg ch-2, turn.

Row 92: Ch 2, work 20 sts, with CC2 work 2 sts, with CC work 14 sts, with CC2 work 2 sts, with MC work 22 sts, hdc in top of beg ch-2, turn.

Row 93: Ch 2, work 22 sts, with CC2 work 1 st, with CC work 15 sts, with CC2 work 2 sts, with MC work 20 sts, hdc in top of beg ch-2, turn.

Row 94: Ch 2, work 21 sts, with CC2 work 1 st, with CC work 15 sts, with CC2 work 1 st, with MC work 22 sts, hdc in top of beg ch-2, turn.

Row 95: Ch 2, work 22 sts, with CC2 work 1 st, with CC work 15 sts, with CC2 work 1 st, with MC work 21 sts, hdc in top of beg ch-2, turn.

Row 96: Ch 2, work 21 sts, with CC2 work 1 st, with CC work 15 sts, with CC2 work 2 sts, with MC work 21 sts, hdc in top of beg ch-2, turn.

Row 97: Ch 2, work 21 sts, with CC2 work 2 sts, with CC work 15 sts, with CC2 work 1 st, with MC work 21 sts, hdc in top of beg ch-2, turn.

Row 98: Ch 2, work 21 sts, with CC2 work 1 st, with CC work 16 sts, with CC2 work 1 st, with MC work 21 sts, hdc in top of beg ch-2, turn.

Row 99: Ch 2, work 21 sts, with CC2 work 1 st, with CC work 16 sts, with CC2 work 1 st, with MC work 21 sts, hdc in top of beg ch-2, turn.

Row 100: Ch 2, work 21 sts, with CC2 work 1 st, with CC work 16 sts, with CC2 work 1 st, with MC work 21 sts, hdc in top of beg ch-2, turn.

Row 101: Ch 2, work 20 sts, with CC2 work 2 sts, with CC work 16 sts, with CC2 work 1 st, with MC work 21 sts, hdc in top of beg ch-2, turn.

Row 102: Ch 2, work 21 sts, with CC2 work 1 st, with CC work 16 sts, with CC2 work 2 sts, with MC work 20 sts, hdc in top of beg ch-2, turn.

Row 103: Ch 2, work 20 sts, with CC2 work 1 st, with CC work 17 sts, with CC2 work 2 sts, with MC work 20 sts, hdc in top of beg ch-2, turn.

Row 104: Ch 2, work 20 sts, with CC2 work 2 sts, with CC work 17 sts, with CC2 work 1 st, with MC work 20 sts, hdc in top of beg ch-2, turn.

Row 105: Ch 2, work 20 sts, with CC2 work 1 st, with CC work 18 sts, with CC2 work 1 st, with MC work 20 sts, hdc in top of beg ch-2, turn.

Row 106: Ch 2, work 20 sts, with CC2 work 1 st, with CC work 18 sts, with CC2 work 1 st, with MC work 20 sts, hdc in top of beg ch-2, turn.

Row 107: Ch 2, work 20 sts, with CC2 work 1 st, with CC work 18 sts, with CC2 work 1 st, with MC work 20 sts, hdc in top of beg ch-2, turn.

Row 108: Ch 2, work 20 sts, with CC2 work 1 st, with CC work 18 sts, with CC2 work 2 sts, with MC work 19 sts, hdc in top of beg ch-2, turn.

Row 109: Ch 2, work 19 sts, with CC2 work 2 sts, with CC work 18 sts, with CC2 work 1 st, with MC work 20 sts, hdc in top of beg ch-2, turn.

Row 110: Ch 2, work 19 sts, with CC2 work 2 sts, with CC work 19 sts, with CC2 work 1 st, with MC work 19 sts, hdc in top of beg ch-2, turn.

Row 111: Ch 2, work 19 sts, with CC2 work 1 st, with CC work 19 sts, with CC2 work 2 sts, with MC work 19 sts, hdc in top of beg ch-2, turn.

Row 112: Ch 2, work 19 sts, with CC2 work 1 st, with CC work 20 sts, with CC2 work 2 sts, with MC work 18 sts, hdc in top of beg ch-2, turn.

Row 113: Ch 2, work 18 sts, with CC2 work 2 sts, with CC work 20 sts, with CC2 work 2 sts, with MC work 18 sts, hdc in top of beg ch-2, turn.

Row 114: Ch 2, work 18 sts, with CC2 work 1 st, with CC work 22 sts, with CC2 work 1 st, with MC work 18 sts, hdc in top of beg ch-2, turn.

Row 115: Ch 2, work 17 sts, with CC2 work 2 sts, with CC work 22 sts, with CC2 work 1 st, with MC work 18 sts, hdc in top of beg ch-2, turn.

Row 116: Ch 2, work 17 sts, with CC2 work 2 sts, with CC work 23 sts, with CC2 work 1 st, with MC work 17 sts, hdc in top of beg ch-2, turn.

Row 117: Ch 2, work 17 sts, with CC2 work 1 st, with CC work 23 sts, with CC2 work 2 sts, with MC work 17 sts, hdc in top of beg ch-2, turn.

Row 118: Ch 2, work 17 sts, with CC2 work 1 st, with CC work 24 sts, with CC2 work 2 sts, with MC work 16 sts, hdc in top of beg ch-2, turn.

Row 119: Ch 2, work 16 sts, with CC2 work 2 sts, with CC work 24 sts, with CC2 work 1 st, with MC work 17 sts, hdc in top of beg ch-2, turn.

Row 120: Ch 2, work 17 sts, with CC2 work 1 st, with CC work 25 sts, with CC2 work 1 st, with MC work 16 sts, hdc in top of beg ch-2, turn.

Row 121: Ch 2, work 16 sts, with CC2 work 1 st, with CC work 25 sts, with CC2 work 1 st, with MC work 17 sts, hdc in top of beg ch-2, turn.

Row 122: Ch 2, work 17 sts, with CC2 work 1 st, with CC work 25 sts, with CC2 work 1 st, with MC work 16 sts, hdc in top of beg ch-2, turn.

Row 123: Ch 2, work 16 sts, with CC2 work 1 st, with CC work 25 sts, with CC2 work 1 st, with MC work 17 sts, hdc in top of beg ch-2, turn.

Row 124: Ch 2, work 17 sts, with CC2 work 2 sts, with CC work 24 sts, with CC2 work 1 st, with MC work 16 sts, hdc in top of beg ch-2, turn.

Row 125: Ch 2, work 16 sts, with CC2 work 1 st, with CC work 24 sts, with CC2 work 1 st, with MC work 18 sts, hdc in top of beg ch-2.

Fasten off all colors.

Edging

Note: *Blanket is reversible up to this point. Decide which side you like as the front and make sure right side is facing you as you work the Edging and Border.*

Rnd 1 (RS): Hold blanket with foundation ch at top, join CC2 in first ch in right-hand corner, ch 1, 3 sc in first ch, sc in each ch across to last ch, 3 sc in last ch, rotate blanket to work in row ends, work 3 sc for every 2 rows across side, rotate blanket to work across top row, 3 sc in first st, sc in each st across to last st, 3 sc in last st, rotate blanket to work in row ends, work 3 sc for every 2 rows across side, join in top of first sc. Fasten off. *(126 sts along top and bottom, 188 sts along each side; 628 sts around blanket)*

Twisting Border
Work same as Twisting Border on page 5. ●

Twisting Border

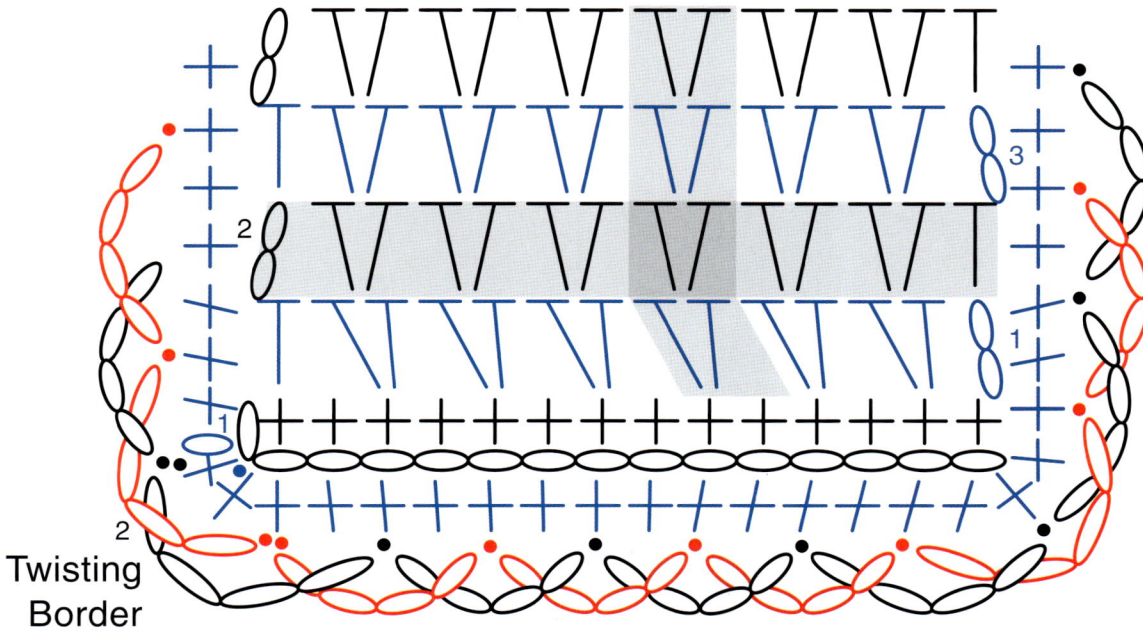

Mermaid Dreams
Reduced Sample of Stitch Diagram
Note: Rep shown in gray.

STITCH KEY

⬭	Chain (ch)
•	Slip stitch (sl st)
+	Single crochet (sc)
⊤	Half double crochet (hdc)
V	Mini V-stitch (mini V-st)

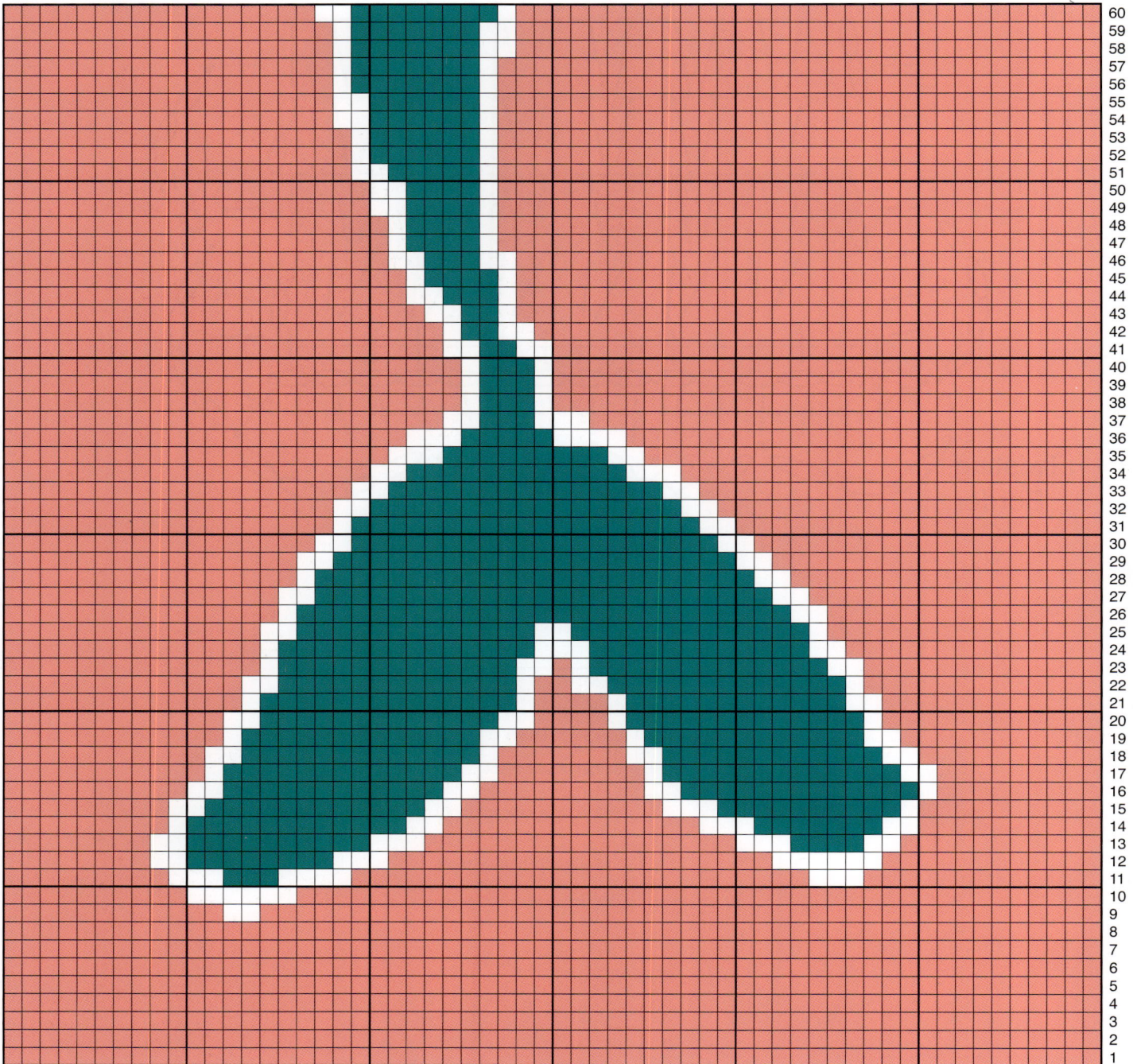

Mermaid Dreams
Chart (A)

COLOR KEY

■	Contrasting Color - Silhouette
□	Contrasting Color 2 - Outline
■	Main Color - Background

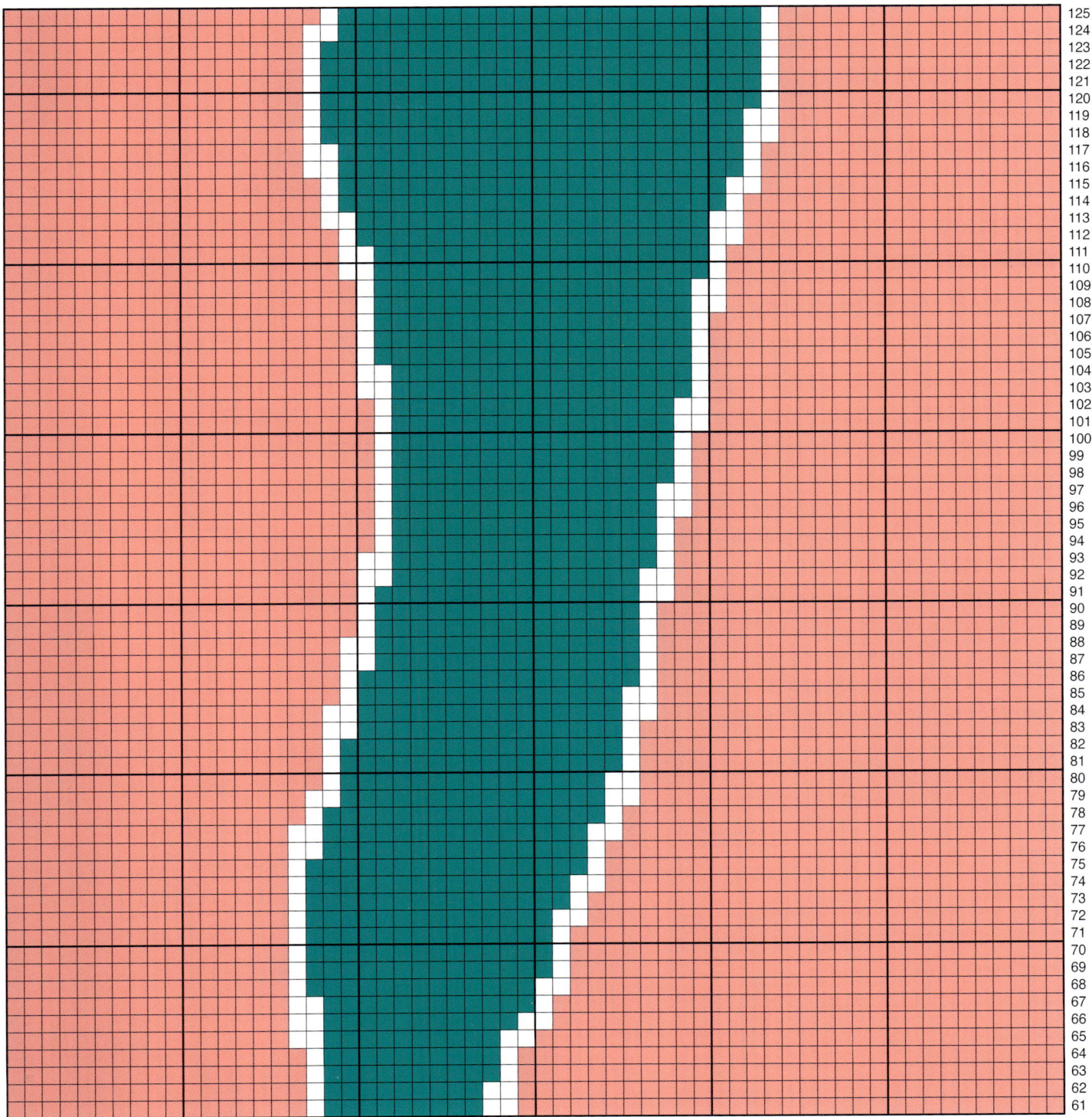

Mermaid Dreams
Chart (B)

Seahorse Splash

Skill Level
◼◼◻◻ **EASY**

Finished Measurements
Approximately 38 inches wide x 48 inches long

Materials
- Red Heart Super Saver medium (worsted) weight acrylic yarn (7 oz/364 yds/198g per skein):
    - 4 skeins #347 light periwinkle (MC)
    - 1 skein #311 white (CC2)
- Red Heart Super Saver Ombré medium (worsted) weight acrylic yarn (10 oz/ 482 yds/283g per skein):
    - 1 skein #3967 sea coral (CC)
- Size I/9/5.5mm crochet hook or size needed to obtain gauge
- Tapestry needle
- Bobbins (optional)

4 MEDIUM

Gauge
15 sts = 4 inches; 11 rows = 4 inches

Pattern Notes
Before beginning, we suggest you read the General Instructions on pages 2–6 for information needed to work the pattern.

Refer to Stitch Diagrams and Color Chart as needed.

All rows begin with MC.

Weave in loose ends as work progresses.

Chain-2 at beginning of row counts as a half double crochet unless otherwise stated.

Special Stitch

Mini V-stitch (mini V-st): 2 hdc in indicated st or sp.

Blanket

Foundation row (WS): With MC, ch 123, sc in 2nd ch from hook and in each rem ch across, turn. *(122 sts)*

Row 1 (RS): Ch 2 *(see Pattern Notes)*, *mini V-st *(see Special Stitch)* in next st, sk next st, rep from * across to last st, hdc in last st, turn. *(60 sts, 2 hdc)*

Row 2: Ch 2, *mini V-st in between hdc of each mini V-st across, hdc in top of beg ch-2, turn.

Rows 3–13: Rep row 2.

Row 14: Ch 2, mini V-st in each of next 28 sts, **changing color** *(see General Instructions)* to CC2 in last leg of last mini V-st, mini V-st between hdc of each of next 7 mini V-sts, changing color to MC in last leg of last mini V-st, mini V-st between hdc of each of next 25 mini V-sts, hdc in top of beg ch-2, turn.

Note: *On following rows, mini V-sts will be referred to as sts.*

Row 15: Ch 2, work 23 sts, with CC2 work 11 sts, with MC work 26 sts, hdc in top of beg ch-2, turn.

Row 16: Ch 2, work 24 sts, with CC2 work 4 sts, with CC work 8 sts, with CC2 work 2 sts, with MC work 22 sts, hdc in top of beg ch-2, turn.

Row 17: Ch 2, work 20 sts, with CC2 work 2 sts, with CC work 13 sts, with CC2 work 2 sts, with MC work 23 sts, hdc in top of beg ch-2, turn.

Row 18: Ch 2, work 22 sts, with CC2 work 2 sts, with CC work 15 sts, with CC2 work 2 sts, with MC work 19 sts, hdc in top of beg ch-2, turn.

Row 19: Ch 2, work 18 sts, with CC2 work 2 sts, with CC work 17 sts, with CC2 work 2 sts, with MC work 21 sts, hdc in top of beg ch-2, turn.

Row 20: Ch 2, work 20 sts, with CC2 work 2 sts, with CC work 19 sts, with CC2 work 2 sts, with MC work 17 sts, hdc in top of beg ch-2, turn.

Row 21: Ch 2, work 16 sts, with CC2 work 2 sts, with CC work 21 sts, with CC2 work 2 sts, with MC work 19 sts, hdc in top of beg ch-2, turn.

Row 22: Ch 2, work 18 sts, with CC2 work 2 sts, with CC work 23 sts, with CC2 work 2 sts, with MC work 15 sts, hdc in top of beg ch-2, turn.

Row 23: Ch 2, work 14 sts, with CC2 work 2 sts, with CC work 11 sts, with CC2 work 3 sts, with CC work 11 sts, with CC2 work 1 st, with MC work 18 sts, hdc in top of beg ch-2, turn.

Row 24: Ch 2, work 17 sts, with CC2 work 1 st, with CC work 10 sts, with CC2 work 7 sts, with CC work 10 sts, with CC2 work 1 st, with MC work 14 sts, hdc in top of beg ch-2, turn.

Row 25: Ch 2, work 13 sts, with CC2 work 2 sts, with CC work 8 sts, with CC2 work 3 sts, with MC work 4 sts, with CC2 work 2 sts, with CC work 10 sts, with CC2 work 2 sts, with MC work 16 sts, hdc in top of beg ch-2, turn.

Row 26: Ch 2, work 16 sts, with CC2 work 1 st, with CC work 10 sts, with CC2 work 2 sts, with MC work 6 sts, with CC2 work 4 sts, with CC work 7 sts, with CC2 work 1 st, with MC work 13 sts, hdc in top of beg ch-2, turn.

Row 27: Ch 2, work 13 sts, with CC2 work 1 st, with CC work 7 sts, with CC2 work 3 sts, with MC work 8 sts, with CC2 work 3 sts, with CC work 8 sts, with CC2 work 2 sts, with MC work 15 sts, hdc in top of beg ch-2, turn.

Row 28: Ch 2, work 15 sts, with CC2 work 2 sts, with CC work 8 sts, with CC2 work 3 sts, with MC work 10 sts, with CC2 work 2 sts, with CC work 6 sts, with CC2 work 1 st, with MC work 13 sts, hdc in top of beg ch-2, turn.

Row 29: Ch 2, work 12 sts, with CC2 work 2 sts, with CC work 5 sts, with CC2 work 3 sts, with MC work 12 sts, with CC2 work 2 sts, with CC work 8 sts, with CC2 work 1 st, with MC work 15 sts, hdc in top of beg ch-2, turn.

Row 30: Ch 2, work 15 sts, with CC2 work 1 st, with CC work 7 sts, with CC2 work 2 sts, with MC work 6 sts, with CC2 work 4 sts, with MC work 4 sts, with CC2 work 2 sts, with CC work 6 sts, with CC2 work 1 st, with MC work 12 sts, hdc in top of beg ch-2, turn.

Row 31: Ch 2, work 12 sts, with CC2 work 1 st, with CC work 5 sts, with CC2 work 2 sts, with MC work 4 sts, with CC2 work 3 sts, with CC work 1 st, with CC2 work 3 sts, with MC work 4 sts, with CC2 work 2 sts, with CC work 7 sts, with CC2 work 2 sts, with MC work 14 sts, hdc in top of beg ch-2, turn.

Row 32: Ch 2, work 14 sts, with CC2 work 2 sts, with CC work 7 sts, with CC2 work 1 st, with MC work 4 sts, with CC2 work 2 sts, with CC work 5 sts, with CC2 work 1 st, with MC work 5 sts, with CC2 work 1 st, with CC work 5 sts, with CC2 work 1 st, with MC work 12 sts, hdc in top of beg ch-2, turn.

Row 33: Ch 2, work 12 sts, with CC2 work 1 st, with CC work 4 sts, with CC2 work 2 sts, with MC work 4 sts, with CC2 work 2 sts, with CC work 6 sts, with CC2 work 2 sts, with MC work 3 sts, with CC2 work 2 sts, with CC work 6 sts, with CC2 work 2 sts, with MC work 14 sts, hdc in top of beg ch-2, turn.

Row 34: Ch 2, work 14 sts, with CC2 work 1 st, with CC work 7 sts, with CC2 work 2 sts, with MC work 2 sts, with CC2 work 2 sts, with CC work 8 sts, with CC2 work 2 sts, with MC work 4 sts, with CC2 work 1 st, with CC work 4 sts, with CC2 work 2 sts, with MC work 11 sts, hdc in top of beg ch-2, turn.

Row 35: Ch 2, work 11 sts, with CC2 work 1 st, with CC work 4 sts, with CC2 work 2 sts, with MC work 4 sts, with CC2 work 1 st, with CC work 10 sts, with CC2 work 1 st, with MC work 3 sts, with CC2 work 1 st, with CC work 7 sts, with CC2 work 1 st, with MC work 14 sts, hdc in top of beg ch-2, turn.

Row 36: Ch 2, work 14 sts, with CC2 work 1 st, with CC work 6 sts, with CC2 work 2 sts, with MC work 3 sts, with CC2 work 1 st, with CC work 3 sts, with CC2 work 5 sts, with CC2 work 2 sts, with CC2 work 1 st, with MC work 4 sts, with CC2 work 2 sts, with CC work 4 sts, with CC2 work 1 st, with MC work 11 sts, hdc in top of beg ch-2, turn.

Row 37: Ch 2, work 11 sts, with CC2 work 1 st, with CC work 4 sts, with CC2 work 1 st, with MC work 4 sts, with CC2 work 1 st, with CC work 3 sts, with CC2 work 2 sts, with MC work 2 sts, with CC2 work 2 sts, with CC work 2 sts, with CC2 work 1 st, with MC work 3 sts, with CC2 work 2 sts, with CC work 6 sts, with CC2 work 1 st, with MC work 14 sts, hdc in top of beg ch-2, turn.

Row 38: Ch 2, work 13 sts, with CC2 work 2 sts, with CC work 6 sts, with CC2 work 2 sts, with MC work 2 sts, with CC2 work 2 sts, with CC work 2 sts, with CC2 work 1 st, with MC work 4 sts, with CC2 work 2 sts, with CC work 2 sts, with CC2 work 2 sts, with MC work 3 sts, with CC2 work 1 st, with CC work 4 sts, with CC2 work 1 st, with MC work 11 sts, hdc in top of beg ch-2, turn.

Row 39: Ch 2, work 11 sts, with CC2 work 1 st, with CC work 4 sts, with CC2 work 1 st, with MC work 3 sts, with CC2 work 1 st, with CC work 2 sts, with CC2 work 2 sts, with MC work 5 sts, with CC2 work 1 st, with CC work 3 sts, with CC2 work 1 st, with MC work 3 sts, with CC2 work 1 st, with CC work 6 sts, with CC2 work 2 sts, with MC work 13 sts, hdc in top of beg ch-2, turn.

Row 40: Ch 2, work 13 sts, with CC2 work 1 st, with CC work 7 sts, with CC2 work 1 st, with MC work 3 sts, with CC2 work 1 st, with CC work 2 sts, with CC2 work 2 sts, with MC work 6 sts, with CC2 work 1 st, with CC work 2 sts, with CC2 work 1 st, with MC work 3 sts, with CC2 work 1 st, with CC work 4 sts, with CC2 work 1 st, with MC work 11 sts, hdc in top of beg ch-2, turn.

Row 41: Ch 2, work 11 sts, with CC2 work 1 st, with CC work 4 sts, with CC2 work 1 st, with MC work 3 sts, with CC2 work 1 st, with CC work 2 sts, with CC2 work 1 st, with MC work 7 sts, with CC2 work 1 st, with CC work 2 sts, with CC2 work 1 st, with MC work 3 sts, with CC2 work 1 st, with CC work 7 sts, with CC2 work 1 st, with MC work 13 sts, hdc in top of beg ch-2, turn.

Row 42: Ch 2, work 13 sts, with CC2 work 1 st, with CC work 7 sts, with CC2 work 1 st, with MC work 3 sts, with CC2 work 1 st, with CC work 2 sts, with CC2 work 1 st, with MC work 6 sts, with CC2 work 2 sts, with CC work 2 sts, with CC2 work 1 st, with MC work 3 sts, with CC2 work 1 st, with CC work 4 sts, with CC2 work 1 st, with MC work 11 sts, hdc in top of beg ch-2, turn.

Row 43: Ch 2, work 11 sts, with CC2 work 1 st, with CC work 4 sts, with CC2 work 1 st, with MC work 3 sts, with CC2 work 1 st, with CC work 3 sts, with CC2 work 1 st, with MC work 6 sts, with CC2 work 1 st, with CC work 2 sts, with CC2 work 1 st, with MC work 3 sts, with CC2 work 1 st, with CC work 7 sts, with CC2 work 1 st, with MC work 13 sts, hdc in top of beg ch-2, turn.

Row 44: Ch 2, work 13 sts, with CC2 work 1 st, with CC work 7 sts, with CC2 work 1 st, with MC work 3 sts, with CC2 work 1 st, with CC work 2 sts, with CC2 work 1 st, with MC work 5 sts, with CC2 work 2 sts, with CC work 2 sts, with CC2 work 2 sts, with MC work 3 sts, with CC2 work 1 st, with CC work 4 sts, with CC2 work 1 st, with MC work 11 sts, hdc in top of beg ch-2, turn.

Row 45: Ch 2, work 11 sts, with CC2 work 1 st, with CC work 4 sts, with CC2 work 1 st, with MC work 4 sts, with CC2 work 1 st, with CC work 3 sts, with CC2 work 2 sts, with MC work 4 sts, with CC2 work 1 st, with CC work 2 sts, with CC2 work 1 st, with MC work 3 sts, with CC2 work 1 st, with CC work 7 sts, with CC2 work 1 st, with MC work 13 sts, hdc in top of beg ch-2, turn.

Row 46: Ch 2, work 12 sts, with CC2 work 2 sts, with CC work 7 sts, with CC2 work 1 st, with MC work 3 sts, with CC2 work 1 st, with CC work 2 sts, with CC2 work 2 sts, with MC work 3 sts, with CC2 work 1 st, with CC work 3 sts, with CC2 work 2 sts, with MC work 4 sts, with CC2 work 1 st, with CC work 4 sts, with CC2 work 1 st, with MC work 11 sts, hdc in top of beg ch-2, turn.

Row 47: Ch 2, work 11 sts, with CC2 work 2 sts, with CC work 3 sts, with CC2 work 1 st, with MC work 6 sts, with CC2 work 1 st, with CC work 2 sts, with CC2 work 1 st, with MC work 3 sts, with CC2 work 1 st, with CC work 3 sts, with CC2 work 1 st, with MC work 3 sts, with CC2 work 1 st, with CC work 7 sts, with CC2 work 2 sts, with MC work 12 sts, hdc in top of beg ch-2, turn.

Row 48: Ch 2, work 12 sts, with CC2 work 1 st, with CC work 8 sts, with CC2 work 1 st, with MC work 3 sts, with CC2 work 1 st, with CC work 3 sts, with CC2 work 2 sts, with MC work 2 sts, with CC2 work 4 sts, with MC work 5 sts, with CC2 work 2 sts, with CC work 3 sts, with CC2 work 1 st, with MC work 12 sts, hdc in top of beg ch-2, turn.

Row 49: Ch 2, work 12 sts, with CC2 work 1 st, with CC work 4 sts, with CC2 work 1 st, with MC work 11 sts, with CC2 work 2 sts, with CC work 2 sts, with CC2 work 2 sts, with MC work 3 sts, with CC2 work 1 st, with CC work 8 sts, with CC2 work 1 st, with MC work 12 sts, hdc in top of beg ch-2, turn.

Row 50: Ch 2, work 12 sts, with CC2 work 1 st, with CC work 8 sts, with CC2 work 2 sts, with MC work 3 sts, with CC2 work 1 st, with CC work 3 sts, with CC2 work 1 st, with MC work 10 sts, with CC2 work 2 sts, with CC work 4 sts, with CC2 work 1 st, with MC work 12 sts, hdc in top of beg ch-2, turn.

Row 51: Ch 2, work 12 sts, with CC2 work 1 st, with CC work 5 sts, with CC2 work 2 sts, with MC work 8 sts, with CC2 work 2 sts, with CC work 3 sts, with CC2 work 1 st, with MC work 3 sts, with CC2 work 1 st, with CC work 9 sts, with CC2 work 1 st, with MC work 12 sts, hdc in top of beg ch-2, turn.

Row 52: Ch 2, work 12 sts, with CC2 work 1 st, with CC work 9 sts, with CC2 work 1 st, with MC work 3 sts, with CC2 work 2 sts, with CC work 2 sts, with CC2 work 2 sts, with MC work 7 sts, with CC2 work 2 sts, with CC work 5 sts, with CC2 work 2 sts, with MC work 12 sts, hdc in top of beg ch-2, turn.

Row 53: Ch 2, work 13 sts, with CC2 work 2 sts, with CC work 4 sts, with CC2 work 3 sts, with MC work 5 sts, with CC2 work 2 sts, with CC work 3 sts, with CC2 work 1 st, with MC work 4 sts, with CC2 work 1 st, with CC work 9 sts, with CC2 work 1 st, with MC work 12 sts, hdc in top of beg ch-2, turn.

Row 54: Ch 2, work 12 sts, with CC2 work 1 st, with CC work 9 sts, with CC2 work 1 st, with MC work 4 sts, with CC2 work 2 sts, with CC work 2 sts, with CC2 work 3 sts, with MC work 2 sts, with CC2 work 4 sts, with CC work 5 sts, with CC2 work 1 st, with MC work 14 sts, hdc in top of beg ch-2, turn.

Row 55: Ch 2, work 14 sts, with CC2 work 2 sts, with CC work 5 sts, with CC2 work 7 sts, with CC work 3 sts, with CC2 work 2 sts, with MC work 3 sts, with CC2 work 2 sts, with CC work 9 sts, with CC2 work 1 st, with MC work 12 sts, hdc in top of beg ch-2, turn.

Row 56: Ch 2, work 12 sts, with CC2 work 1 st, with CC work 9 sts, with CC2 work 2 sts, with MC work 4 sts, with CC2 work 1 st, with CC work 4 sts, with CC2 work 4 sts, with CC work 6 sts, with CC2 work 2 sts, with MC work 15 sts, hdc in top of beg ch-2, turn.

Row 57: Ch 2, work 16 sts, with CC2 work 2 sts, with CC work 13 sts, with CC2 work 1 st, with MC work 4 sts, with CC2 work 2 sts, with CC work 9 sts, with CC2 work 1 st, with MC work 12 sts, hdc in top of beg ch-2, turn.

Row 58: Ch 2, work 12 sts, with CC2 work 1 st, with CC work 10 sts, with CC2 work 1 st, with MC work 4 sts, with CC2 work 2 sts, with CC work 11 sts, with CC2 work 3 sts, with MC work 16 sts, hdc in top of beg ch-2, turn.

Row 59: Ch 2, work 18 sts, with CC2 work 3 sts, with CC work 8 sts, with CC2 work 2 sts, with MC work 4 sts, with CC2 work 2 sts, with CC work 10 sts, with CC2 work 1 st, with MC work 12 sts, hdc in top of beg ch-2, turn.

Row 60: Ch 2, work 12 sts, with CC2 work 2 sts, with CC work 9 sts, with CC2 work 2 sts, with MC work 5 sts, with CC2 work 2 sts, with CC work 6 sts, with CC2 work 3 sts, with MC work 19 sts, hdc in top of beg ch-2, turn.

Row 61: Ch 2, work 21 sts, with CC2 work 8 sts, with MC work 6 sts, with CC2 work 1 st, with CC work 10 sts, with CC2 work 2 sts, with MC work 12 sts, hdc in top of beg ch-2, turn.

Row 62: Ch 2, work 12 sts, with CC2 work 2 sts, with CC work 10 sts, with CC2 work 1 st, with MC work 7 sts, with CC2 work 5 sts, with MC work 23, hdc in top of beg ch-2, turn.

Row 63: Ch 2, work 34 sts, with CC2 work 2 sts, with CC work 10 sts, with CC2 work 1 st, with MC work 13 sts, hdc in top of beg ch-2, turn.

Row 64: Ch 2, work 13 sts, with CC2 work 2 sts, with CC work 9 sts, with CC2 work 2 sts, with MC work 34 sts, hdc in top of beg ch-2, turn.

Row 65: Ch 2, work 34 sts, with CC2 work 1 st, with CC work 10 sts, with CC2 work 2 sts, with MC work 13 sts, hdc in top of beg ch-2, turn.

Row 66: Ch 2, work 13 sts, with CC2 work 2 sts, with CC work 10 sts, with CC2 work 2 sts, with MC work 33 sts, hdc in top of beg ch-2, turn.

Row 67: Ch 2, work 33 sts, with CC2 work 2 sts, with CC work 10 sts, with CC2 work 2 sts, with MC work 13 sts, hdc in top of beg ch-2, turn.

Row 68: Ch 2, work 14 sts, with CC2 work 1 st, with CC work 11 sts, with CC2 work 1 st, with MC work 33 sts, hdc in top of beg ch-2, turn.

Row 69: Ch 2, work 33 sts, with CC2 work 1 st, with CC work 10 sts, with CC2 work 2 sts, with MC work 14 sts, hdc in top of beg ch-2, turn.

Row 70: Ch 2, work 14 sts, with CC2 work 2 sts, with CC work 10 sts, with CC2 work 2 sts, with MC work 32 sts, hdc in top of beg ch-2, turn.

Row 71: Ch 2, work 32 sts, with CC2 work 1 st, with CC work 11 sts, with CC2 work 2 sts, with MC work 14 sts, hdc in top of beg ch-2, turn.

Row 72: Ch 2, work 15 sts, with CC2 work 1 st, with CC work 11 sts, with CC2 work 2 sts, with MC work 31 sts, hdc in top of beg ch-2, turn.

Row 73: Ch 2, work 31 sts, with CC2 work 2 sts, with CC work 11 sts, with CC2 work 1 st, with MC work 15 sts, hdc in top of beg ch-2, turn.

Row 74: Ch 2, work 15 sts, with CC2 work 1 st, with CC work 12 sts, with CC2 work 1 st, with MC work 31 sts, hdc in top of beg ch-2, turn.

Row 75: Ch 2, work 31 sts, with CC2 work 1 st, with CC work 11 sts, with CC2 work 2 sts, with MC work 15 sts, hdc in top of beg ch-2, turn.

Row 76: Ch 2, work 15 sts, with CC2 work 2 sts, with CC work 11 sts, with CC2 work 2 sts, with MC work 30 sts, hdc in top of beg ch-2, turn.

Row 77: Ch 2, work 30 sts, with CC2 work 1 st, with CC work 12 sts, with CC2 work 2 sts, with MC work 15 sts, hdc in top of beg ch-2, turn.

Row 78: Ch 2, work 16 sts, with CC2 work 1 st, with CC work 12 sts, with CC2 work 1 st, with MC work 30 sts, hdc in top of beg ch-2, turn.

Row 79: Ch 2, work 29 sts, with CC2 work 2 sts, with CC work 12 sts, with CC2 work 1 st, with MC work 16 sts, hdc in top of beg ch-2, turn.

Row 80: Ch 2, work 16 sts, with CC2 work 1 st, with CC work 13 sts, with CC2 work 1 st, with MC work 29 sts, hdc in top of beg ch-2, turn.

Row 81: Ch 2, work 28 sts, with CC2 work 2 sts, with CC work 12 sts, with CC2 work 2 sts, with MC work 16 sts, hdc in top of beg ch-2, turn.

Row 82: Ch 2, work 16 sts, with CC2 work 2 sts, with CC work 13 sts, with CC2 work 2 sts, with MC work 27 sts, hdc in top of beg ch-2, turn.

Row 83: Ch 2, work 27 sts, with CC2 work 1 st, with CC work 14 sts, with CC2 work 2 sts, with MC work 16 sts, hdc in top of beg ch-2, turn.

Row 84: Ch 2, work 17 sts, with CC2 work 2 sts, with CC work 13 sts, with CC2 work 1 st, with MC work 27 sts, hdc in top of beg ch-2, turn.

Row 85: Ch 2, work 26 sts, with CC2 work 1 st, with CC work 14 sts, with CC2 work 2 sts, with MC work 17 sts, hdc in top of beg ch-2, turn.

Row 86: Ch 2, work 17 sts, with CC2 work 2 sts, with CC work 14 sts, with CC2 work 2 sts, with MC work 25 sts, hdc in top of beg ch-2, turn.

Row 87: Ch 2, work 25 sts, with CC2 work 1 st, with CC work 15 sts, with CC2 work 1 st, with MC work 18 sts, hdc in top of beg ch-2, turn.

Row 88: Ch 2, work 18 sts, with CC2 work 2 sts, with CC work 14 sts, with CC2 work 2 sts, with MC work 24 sts, hdc in top of beg ch-2, turn.

Row 89: Ch 2, work 24 sts, with CC2 work 1 st, with CC work 15 sts, with CC2 work 2 sts, with MC work 18 sts, hdc in top of beg ch-2, turn.

Row 90: Ch 2, work 18 sts, with CC2 work 2 sts, with CC work 15 sts, with CC2 work 2 sts, with MC work 23 sts, hdc in top of beg ch-2, turn.

Row 91: Ch 2, work 23 sts, with CC2 work 1 st, with CC work 16 sts, with CC2 work 1 st, with MC work 19 sts, hdc in top of beg ch-2, turn.

Row 92: Ch 2, work 19 sts, with CC2 work 1 st, with CC work 16 sts, with CC2 work 2 sts, with MC work 22 sts, hdc in top of beg ch-2, turn.

Row 93: Ch 2, work 22 sts, with CC2 work 1 st, with CC work 16 sts, with CC2 work 2 sts, with MC work 19 sts, hdc in top of beg ch-2, turn.

Row 94: Ch 2, work 19 sts, with CC2 work 2 sts, with CC work 16 sts, with CC2 work 2 sts, with MC work 21 sts, hdc in top of beg ch-2, turn.

Row 95: Ch 2, work 21 sts, with CC2 work 1 st, with CC work 17 sts, with CC2 work 1 st, with MC work 20 sts, hdc in top of beg ch-2, turn.

Row 96: Ch 2, work 15 sts, with CC2 work 2 sts, with MC work 3 sts, with CC2 work 1 st, with CC work 17 sts, with CC2 work 2 sts, with MC work 20 sts, hdc in top of beg ch-2, turn.

Row 97: Ch 2, work 20 sts, with CC2 work 1 st, with CC work 17 sts, with CC2 work 2 sts, with MC work 2 sts, with CC2 work 4 sts, with MC work 14 sts, hdc in top of beg ch-2, turn.

Row 98: Ch 2, work 14 sts, with CC2 work 1 st, with CC work 2 sts, with CC2 work 2 sts, with MC work 2 sts, with CC2 work 1 st, with CC work 17 sts, with CC2 work 2 sts, with MC work 19 sts, hdc in top of beg ch-2, turn.

Row 99: Ch 2, work 19 sts, with CC2 work 1 st, with CC work 18 sts, with CC2 work 1 st, with MC work 2 sts, with CC2 work 1 st, with CC work 3 sts, with CC2 work 1 st, with MC work 14 sts, hdc in top of beg ch-2, turn.

Row 100: Ch 2, work 14 sts, with CC2 work 2 sts, with CC work 3 sts, with CC2 work 1 st, with MC work 1 st, with CC2 work 2 sts, with CC work 17 sts, with CC2 work 2 sts, with MC work 18 sts, hdc in top of beg ch-2, turn.

Row 101: Ch 2, work 18 sts, with CC2 work 1 st, with CC work 18 sts, with CC2 work 2 sts, with MC work 1 st, with CC2 work 1 st, with CC work 3 sts, with CC2 work 1 st, with MC work 15 sts, hdc in top of beg ch-2, turn.

Row 102: Ch 2, work 15 sts, with CC2 work 1 st, with CC work 3 sts, with CC2 work 1 st, with MC work 1 st, with CC2 work 2 sts, with CC work 18 sts, with CC2 work 2 sts, with MC work 17 sts, hdc in top of beg ch-2, turn.

Row 103: Ch 2, work 17 sts, with CC2 work 1 st, with CC work 19 sts, with CC2 work 4 sts, with CC work 2 sts, with CC2 work 1 st, with MC work 16 sts, hdc in top of beg ch-2, turn.

Row 104: Ch 2, work 16 sts, with CC2 work 1 st, with CC work 3 sts, with CC2 work 2 sts, with CC work 20 sts, with CC2 work 1 st, with MC work 17 sts, hdc in top of beg ch-2, turn.

Row 105: Ch 2, work 16 sts, with CC2 work 2 sts, with CC work 21 sts, with CC2 work 1 st, with CC work 2 sts, with CC2 work 2 sts, with MC work 16 sts, hdc in top of beg ch-2, turn.

Row 106: Ch 2, work 16 sts, with CC2 work 2 sts, with CC work 24 sts, with CC2 work 2 sts, with MC work 16 sts, hdc in top of beg ch-2, turn.

Row 107: Ch 2, work 16 sts, with CC2 work 1 st, with CC work 26 sts, with CC2 work 1 st, with MC work 16 sts, hdc in top of beg ch-2, turn.

Row 108: Ch 2, work 15 sts, with CC2 work 2 sts, with CC work 26 sts, with CC2 work 1 st, with MC work 16 sts, hdc in top of beg ch-2, turn.

Row 109: Ch 2, work 15 sts, with CC2 work 2 sts, with CC work 27 sts, with CC2 work 1 st, with MC work 15 sts, hdc in top of beg ch-2, turn.

Row 110: Ch 2, work 14 sts, with CC2 work 2 sts, with CC work 27 sts, with CC2 work 2 sts, with MC work 15 sts, hdc in top of beg ch-2, turn.

Row 111: Ch 2, work 15 sts, with CC2 work 1 st, with CC work 28 sts, with CC2 work 2 sts, with MC work 14 sts, hdc in top of beg ch-2, turn.

Row 112: Ch 2, work 14 sts, with CC2 work 2 sts, with CC work 28 sts, with CC2 work 2 sts, with MC work 14 sts, hdc in top of beg ch-2, turn.

Row 113: Ch 2, work 14 sts, with CC2 work 2 sts, with CC work 28 sts, with CC2 work 2 sts, with MC work 14 sts, hdc in top of beg ch-2, turn.

Row 114: Ch 2, work 15 sts, with CC2 work 1 st, with CC work 28 sts, with CC2 work 2 sts, with MC work 14 sts, hdc in top of beg ch-2, turn.

Row 115: Ch 2, work 14 sts, with CC2 work 2 sts, with CC work 27 sts, with CC2 work 2 sts, with MC work 15 sts, hdc in top of beg ch-2, turn.

Row 116: Ch 2, work 16 sts, with CC2 work 2 sts, with CC work 26 sts, with CC2 work 2 sts, with MC work 14 sts, hdc in top of beg ch-2, turn.

Row 117: Ch 2, work 14 sts, with CC2 work 2 sts, with CC work 26 sts, with CC2 work 1 st, with MC work 17 sts, hdc in top of beg ch-2, turn.

Row 118: Ch 2, work 17 sts, with CC2 work 1 st, with CC work 26 sts, with CC2 work 2 sts, with MC work 14 sts, hdc in top of beg ch-2, turn.

Row 119: Ch 2, work 14 sts, with CC2 work 2 sts, with CC work 22 sts, with CC2 work 1 st, with CC work 4 sts, with CC2 work 1 st, with MC work 16 sts, hdc in top of beg ch-2, turn.

Row 120: Ch 2, work 15 sts, with CC2 work 2 sts, with CC work 3 sts, with CC2 work 3 sts, with CC work 21 sts, with CC2 work 2 sts, with MC work 14 sts, hdc in top of beg ch-2, turn.

Row 121: Ch 2, work 14 sts, with CC2 work 2 sts, with CC work 21 sts, with CC2 work 4 sts, with CC work 3 sts, with CC2 work 1 st, with MC work 15 sts, hdc in top of beg ch-2, turn.

Row 122: Ch 2, work 14 sts, with CC2 work 2 sts, with CC work 3 sts, with CC2 work 1 st, with MC work 2 sts, with CC2 work 2 sts, with CC work 20 sts, with CC2 work 2 sts, with MC work 14 sts, hdc in top of beg ch-2, turn.

Row 123: Ch 2, work 14 sts, with CC2 work 2 sts, with CC work 20 sts, with CC2 work 1 st, with MC work 3 sts, with CC2 work 1 st, with CC work 4 sts, with CC2 work 1 st, with MC work 14 sts, hdc in top of beg ch-2, turn.

Row 124: Ch 2, work 13 sts, with CC2 work 2 sts, with CC work 3 sts, with CC2 work 2 sts, with MC work 3 sts, with CC2 work 1 st, with CC work 20 sts, with CC2 work 2 sts, with MC work 14 sts, hdc in top of beg ch-2, turn.

Row 125: Ch 2, work 15 sts, with CC2 work 2 sts, with CC work 19 sts, with CC2 work 1 st, with MC work 4 sts, with CC2 work 2 sts, with CC work 2 sts, with CC2 work 2 sts, with MC work 13 sts, hdc in top of beg ch-2.

Fasten off all colors.

Edging

Note: *Blanket is reversible up to this point. Decide which side you like as the front and make sure right side is facing you as you work the Edging and Border.*

Rnd 1 (RS): Hold blanket with foundation ch at top, join CC2 in first ch in right-hand corner, ch 1, 3 sc in first ch, sc in each ch across to last ch, 3 sc in last ch, rotate blanket to work in row ends, work 3 sc for every 2 rows across side, rotate blanket to work across top row, 3 sc in first st, sc in each st across to last st, 3 sc in last st, rotate blanket to work in row ends, work 3 sc for every 2 rows across side, join in top of first sc. Fasten off. *(126 sts along top and bottom, 188 sts along each side; 628 sts around blanket)*

Twisting Border

Work same as Twisting Border on page 5. ●

Twisting Border

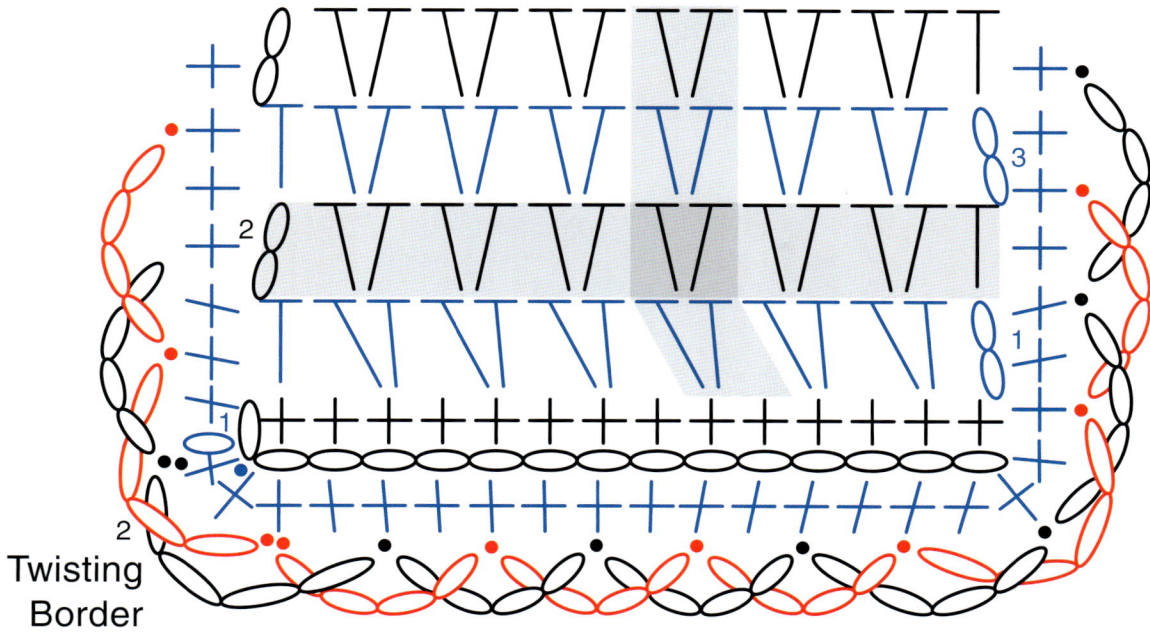

Seahorse Splash
Reduced Sample of Stitch Diagram
Note: Rep shown in gray.

STITCH KEY	
⬭	Chain (ch)
•	Slip stitch (sl st)
+	Single crochet (sc)
⊤	Half double crochet (hdc)
⋁	Mini V-stitch (mini V-st)

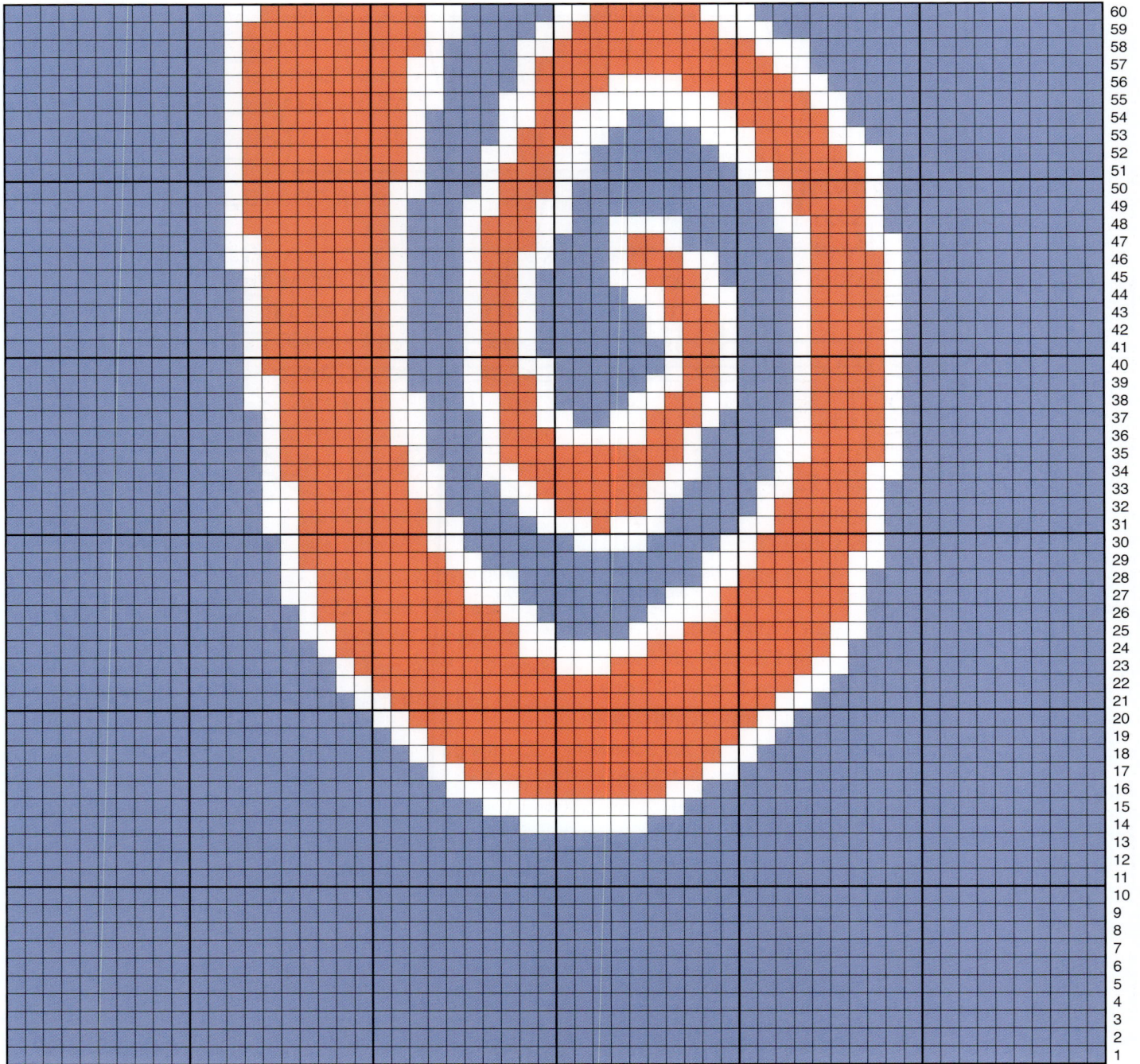

Seahorse Splash
Chart (A)

COLOR KEY
- ■ Contrasting Color - Silhouette
- □ Contrasting Color 2 - Outline
- ■ Main Color - Background

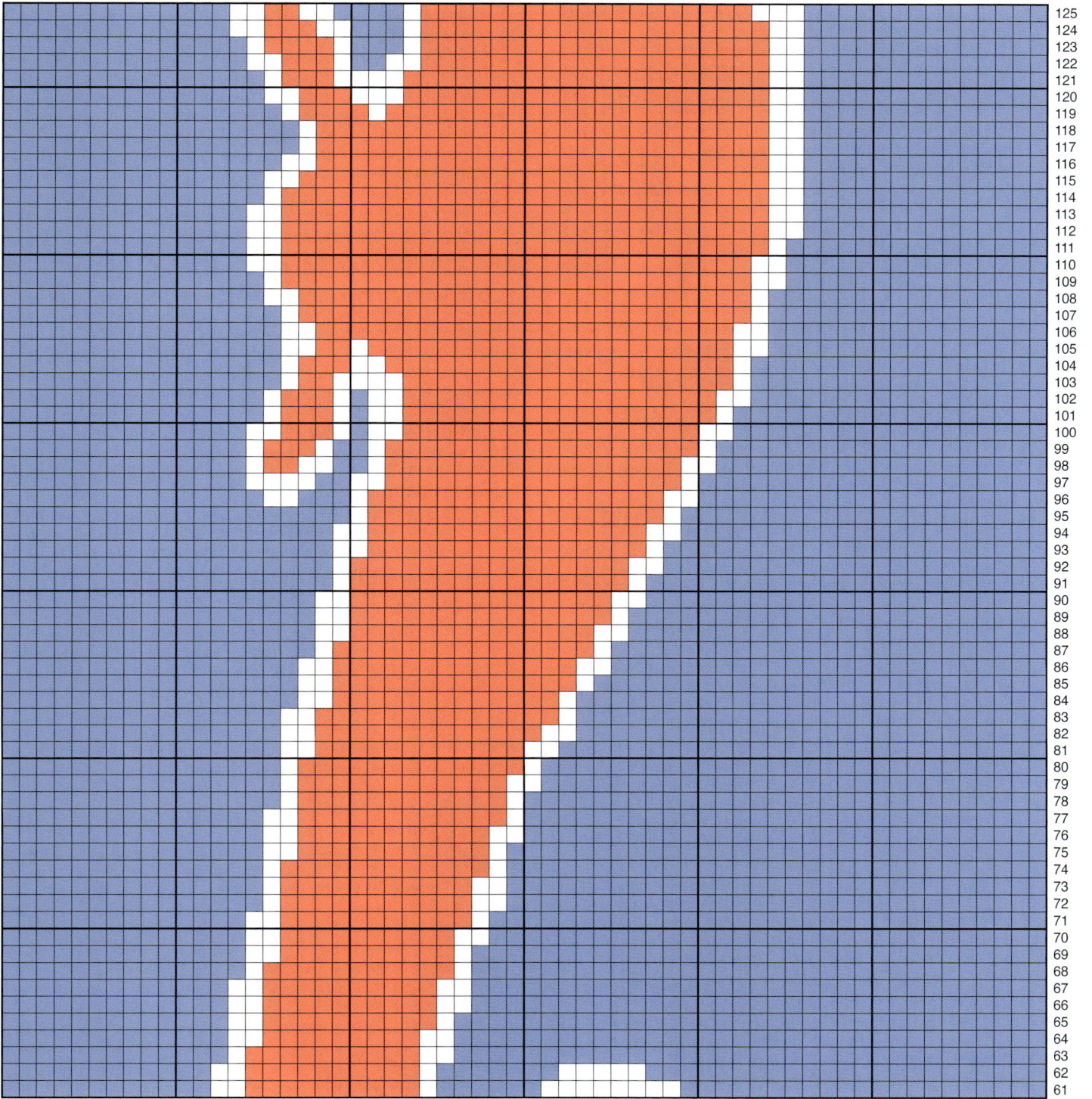

Seahorse Splash
Chart (B)

Shark Bait

Skill Level

◼◼◻◻ **EASY**

Finished Measurements

Approximately 38 inches wide x 48 inches long

Materials

- Red Heart Super Saver Ombré medium (worsted) weight acrylic yarn (10 oz/482 yds/283g per skein):

  4 MEDIUM

    3 skeins #3963 Baja blue (MC)
- Red Heart Super Saver medium (worsted) weight acrylic yarn (7 oz/364 yds/198g per skein):
    2 skeins #341 light grey (CC)
    1 skein #3950 charcoal (CC2)
- Size I/9/5.5mm crochet hook or size needed to obtain gauge
- Tapestry needle
- Bobbins (optional)

Gauge

15 sts = 4 inches; 11 rows = 4 inches

Pattern Notes

Before beginning, we suggest you read the General Instructions on pages 2–6 for information needed to work the pattern.

Refer to Stitch Diagrams and Color Chart as needed.

All rows begin with MC.

Weave in loose ends as work progresses.

Chain-2 at beginning of row counts as a half double crochet unless otherwise stated.

Special Stitch

Mini V-stitch (mini V-st): 2 hdc in indicated st or sp.

Blanket

Foundation row (WS): With MC, ch 123, sc in 2nd ch from hook and in each rem ch across, turn. *(122 sc)*

Row 1 (RS): Ch 2 *(see Pattern Notes)*, ***mini V-st** *(see Special Stitch)* in next st, sk next st, rep from * across to last st, hdc in last st, turn. *(60 sts, 2 hdc)*

Row 2: Ch 2, *mini V-st in between hdc of each mini V-st across, hdc in top of beg ch-2, turn.

Rows 3–6: Rep row 2.

Row 7: Ch 2, mini V-st in each of next 12 sts, **changing color** *(see General Instructions)* to CC2 in last leg of last mini V-st, mini V-st between hdc of each of next 2 mini V-sts, changing color to MC in last leg of last mini V-st, mini V-st between hdc of each of next 46 mini V-sts, hdc in top of beg ch-2, turn.

Note: On following rows, mini V-sts will be referred to as sts.

Row 8: Ch 2, work 45 sts, with CC2 work 3 sts, with MC work 12 sts, hdc in top of beg ch-2, turn.

Row 9: Ch 2, work 12 sts, with CC2 work 1 st, with CC work 1 st, with CC2 work 2 sts, with MC work 44 sts, hdc in top of beg ch-2, turn.

Row 10: Ch 2, work 13 sts, with CC2 work 2 sts, with MC work 28 sts, with CC2 work 2 sts, with CC work 2 sts, with CC2 work 1 st, with MC work 12 sts, hdc in top of beg ch-2, turn.

Row 11: Ch 2, work 12 sts, with CC2 work 2 sts, with CC work 2 sts, with CC2 work 2 sts, with MC work 25 sts, with CC2 work 4 sts, with MC work 13 sts, hdc in top of beg ch-2, turn.

Row 12: Ch 2, work 13 sts, with CC2 work 1 st, with CC work 2 sts, with CC2 work 1 st, with MC work 24 sts, with CC2 work 2 sts, with CC work 3 sts, with CC2 work 1 st, with MC work 13 sts, hdc in top of beg ch-2, turn.

Row 13: Ch 2, work 13 sts, with CC2 work 2 sts, with CC work 3 sts, with CC2 work 2 sts, with MC work 22 sts, with CC2 work 2 sts, with CC work 2 sts, with CC2 work 1 st, with MC work 13 sts, hdc in top of beg ch-2, turn.

Row 14: Ch 2, work 13 sts, with CC2 work 2 sts, with CC work 2 sts, with CC2 work 2 sts, with MC work 20 sts, with CC2 work 2 sts, with CC work 3 sts, with CC2 work 2 sts, with MC work 14 sts, hdc in top of beg ch-2, turn.

Row 15: Ch 2, work 15 sts, with CC2 work 1 st, with CC work 4 sts, with CC2 work 2 sts, with MC work 18 sts, with CC2 work 2 sts, with CC work 3 sts, with CC2 work 1 st, with MC work 14 sts, hdc in top of beg ch-2, turn.

Row 16: Ch 2, work 14 sts, with CC2 work 2 sts, with CC work 3 sts, with CC2 work 2 sts, with MC work 16 sts, with CC2 work 2 sts, with CC work 5 sts, with CC2 work 1 st, with MC work 15 sts, hdc in top of beg ch-2, turn.

Row 17: Ch 2, work 15 sts, with CC2 work 2 sts, with CC work 5 sts, with CC2 work 2 sts, with MC work 14 sts, with CC2 work 2 sts, with CC work 4 sts, with CC2 work 1 st, with MC work 15 sts, hdc in top of beg ch-2, turn.

Row 18: Ch 2, work 15 sts, with CC2 work 2 sts, with CC work 4 sts, with CC2 work 3 sts, with MC work 10 sts, with CC2 work 3 sts, with CC work 5 sts, with CC2 work 2 sts, with MC work 16 sts, hdc in top of beg ch-2, turn.

Row 19: Ch 2, work 17 sts, with CC2 work 1 st, with CC work 6 sts, with CC2 work 3 sts, with MC work 8 sts, with CC2 work 2 sts, with CC work 6 sts, with CC2 work 1 st, with MC work 16 sts, hdc in top of beg ch-2, turn.

Row 20: Ch 2, work 16 sts, with CC2 work 2 sts, with CC work 6 sts, with CC2 work 10 sts, with CC work 7 sts, with CC2 work 2 sts, with MC work 17 sts, hdc in top of beg ch-2, turn.

Row 21: Ch 2, work 18 sts, with CC2 work 2 sts, with CC work 7 sts, with CC2 work 7 sts, with CC work 7 sts, with CC2 work 2 sts, with MC work 17 sts, hdc in top of beg ch-2, turn.

Row 22: Ch 2, work 18 sts, with CC2 work 2 sts, with CC work 20 sts, with CC2 work 1 st, with MC work 19 sts, hdc in top of beg ch-2, turn.

Row 23: Ch 2, work 19 sts, with CC2 work 2 sts, with CC work 18 sts, with CC2 work 2 sts, with MC work 19 sts, hdc in top of beg ch-2, turn.

Row 24: Ch 2, work 20 sts, with CC2 work 1 st, with CC work 18 sts, with CC2 work 1 st, with MC work 20 sts, hdc in top of beg ch-2, turn.

Row 25: Ch 2, work 20 sts, with CC2 work 2 sts, with CC work 16 sts, with CC2 work 2 sts, with MC work 20 sts, hdc in top of beg ch-2, turn.

Row 26: Ch 2, work 21 sts, with CC2 work 2 sts, with CC work 14 sts, with CC2 work 2 sts, with MC work 21 sts, hdc in top of beg ch-2, turn.

Row 27: Ch 2, work 22 sts, with CC2 work 3 sts, with CC work 11 sts, with CC2 work 2 sts, with MC work 22 sts, hdc in top of beg ch-2, turn.

Row 28: Ch 2, work 23 sts, with CC2 work 3 sts, with CC work 8 sts, with CC2 work 2 sts, with MC work 24 sts, hdc in top of beg ch-2, turn.

Row 29: Ch 2, work 25 sts, with CC2 work 2 sts, with CC work 4 sts, with CC2 work 4 sts, with MC work 25 sts, hdc in top of beg ch-2, turn.

Row 30: Ch 2, work 26 sts, with CC2 work 4 sts, with CC work 3 sts, with CC2 work 1 st, with MC work 26 sts, hdc in top of beg ch-2, turn.

Row 31: Ch 2, work 26 sts, with CC2 work 1 st, with CC work 3 sts, with CC2 work 1 st, with MC work 29 sts, hdc in top of beg ch-2, turn.

Row 32: Ch 2, work 29 sts, with CC2 work 1 st, with CC work 3 sts, with CC2 work 1 st, with MC work 26 sts, hdc in top of beg ch-2, turn.

Row 33: Ch 2, work 25 sts, with CC2 work 2 sts, with CC work 3 sts, with CC2 work 2 sts, with MC work 28 sts, hdc in top of beg ch-2, turn.

Row 34: Ch 2, work 28 sts, with CC2 work 2 sts, with CC work 3 sts, with CC2 work 2 sts, with MC work 25 sts, hdc in top of beg ch-2, turn.

Row 35: Ch 2, work 25 sts, with CC2 work 1 st, with CC work 5 sts, with CC2 work 1 st, with MC work 28 sts, hdc in top of beg ch-2, turn.

Row 36: Ch 2, work 27 sts, with CC2 work 2 sts, with CC work 5 sts, with CC2 work 1 st, with MC work 25 sts, hdc in top of beg ch-2, turn.

Row 37: Ch 2, work 24 sts, with CC2 work 2 sts, with CC work 6 sts, with CC2 work 1 st, with MC work 27 sts, hdc in top of beg ch-2, turn.

Row 38: Ch 2, work 27 sts, with CC2 work 1 st, with CC work 6 sts, with CC2 work 2 sts, with MC work 24 sts, hdc in top of beg ch-2, turn.

Row 39: Ch 2, work 23 sts, with CC2 work 2 sts, with CC work 7 sts, with CC2 work 1 st, with MC work 27 sts, hdc in top of beg ch-2, turn.

Row 40: Ch 2, work 26 sts, with CC2 work 2 sts, with CC work 7 sts, with CC2 work 2 sts, with MC work 23 sts, hdc in top of beg ch-2, turn.

Row 41: Ch 2, work 23 sts, with CC2 work 1 st, with CC work 8 sts, with CC2 work 2 sts, with MC work 26 sts, hdc in top of beg ch-2, turn.

Row 42: Ch 2, work 26 sts, with CC2 work 2 sts, with CC work 8 sts, with CC2 work 1 st, with MC work 23 sts, hdc in top of beg ch-2, turn.

Row 43: Ch 2, work 23 sts, with CC2 work 1 st, with CC work 9 sts, with CC2 work 1 st, with MC work 26 sts, hdc in top of beg ch-2, turn.

Row 44: Ch 2, work 26 sts, with CC2 work 1 st, with CC work 9 sts, with CC2 work 2 sts, with MC work 22 sts, hdc in top of beg ch-2, turn.

Row 45: Ch 2, work 22 sts, with CC2 work 2 sts, with CC work 9 sts, with CC2 work 1 st, with MC work 26 sts, hdc in top of beg ch-2, turn.

Row 46: Ch 2, work 26 sts, with CC2 work 1 st, with CC work 9 sts, with CC2 work 2 sts, with MC work 22 sts, hdc in top of beg ch-2, turn.

Row 47: Ch 2, work 22 sts, with CC2 work 1 st, with CC work 10 sts, with CC2 work 2 sts, with MC work 25 sts, hdc in top of beg ch-2, turn.

Row 48: Ch 2, work 25 sts, with CC2 work 1 st, with CC work 11 sts, with CC2 work 2 sts, with MC work 21 sts, hdc in top of beg ch-2, turn.

Row 49: Ch 2, work 21 sts, with CC2 work 2 sts, with CC work 11 sts, with CC2 work 1 st, with MC work 25 sts, hdc in top of beg ch-2, turn.

Row 50: Ch 2, work 25 sts, with CC2 work 1 st, with CC work 12 sts, with CC2 work 1 st, with MC work 21 sts, hdc in top of beg ch-2, turn.

Row 51: Ch 2, work 21 sts, with CC2 work 1 st, with CC work 12 sts, with CC2 work 1 st, with MC work 25 sts, hdc in top of beg ch-2, turn.

Row 52: Ch 2, work 25 sts, with CC2 work 1 st, with CC work 12 sts, with CC2 work 1 st, with MC work 21 sts, hdc in top of beg ch-2, turn.

Row 53: Ch 2, work 21 sts, with CC2 work 1 st, with CC work 12 sts, with CC2 work 1 st, with MC work 25 sts, hdc in top of beg ch-2, turn.

Row 54: Ch 2, work 24 sts, with CC2 work 2 sts, with CC work 12 sts, with CC2 work 2 sts, with MC work 20 sts, hdc in top of beg ch-2, turn.

Row 55: Ch 2, work 20 sts, with CC2 work 2 sts, with CC work 12 sts, with CC2 work 2 sts, with MC work 24 sts, hdc in top of beg ch-2, turn.

Row 56: Ch 2, work 24 sts, with CC2 work 1 st, with CC work 14 sts, with CC2 work 1 st, with MC work 20 sts, hdc in top of beg ch-2, turn.

Row 57: Ch 2, work 20 sts, with CC2 work 1 st, with CC work 14 sts, with CC2 work 1 st, with MC work 24 sts, hdc in top of beg ch-2, turn.

Row 58: Ch 2, work 24 sts, with CC2 work 1 st, with CC work 14 sts, with CC2 work 1 st, with MC work 20 sts, hdc in top of beg ch-2, turn.

Row 59: Ch 2, work 20 sts, with CC2 work 1 st, with CC work 14 sts, with CC2 work 2 sts, with MC work 23 sts, hdc in top of beg ch-2, turn.

Row 60: Ch 2, work 23 sts, with CC2 work 1 st, with CC work 15 sts, with CC2 work 2 sts, with MC work 19 sts, hdc in top of beg ch-2, turn.

Row 61: Ch 2, work 19 sts, with CC2 work 1 st, with CC work 16 sts, with CC2 work 1 st, with MC work 23 sts, hdc in top of beg ch-2, turn.

Row 62: Ch 2, work 23 sts, with CC2 work 1 st, with CC work 16 sts, with CC2 work 1 st, with MC work 19 sts, hdc in top of beg ch-2, turn.

Row 63: Ch 2, work 19 sts, with CC2 work 1 st, with CC work 16 sts, with CC2 work 1 st, with MC work 23 sts, hdc in top of beg ch-2, turn.

Row 64: Ch 2, work 22 sts, with CC2 work 2 sts, with CC work 16 sts, with CC2 work 2 sts, with MC work 18 sts, hdc in top of beg ch-2, turn.

Row 65: Ch 2, work 18 sts, with CC2 work 2 sts, with CC work 16 sts, with CC2 work 2 sts, with MC work 22 sts, hdc in top of beg ch-2, turn.

Row 66: Ch 2, work 22 sts, with CC2 work 1 st, with CC work 17 sts, with CC2 work 2 sts, with MC work 18 sts, hdc in top of beg ch-2, turn.

Row 67: Ch 2, work 18 sts, with CC2 work 1 st, with CC work 18 sts, with CC2 work 1 st, with MC work 22 sts, hdc in top of beg ch-2, turn.

Row 68: Ch 2, work 22 sts, with CC2 work 1 st, with CC work 18 sts, with CC2 work 1 st, with MC work 18 sts, hdc in top of beg ch-2, turn.

Row 69: Ch 2, work 18 sts, with CC2 work 1 st, with CC work 18 sts, with CC2 work 1 st, with MC work 22 sts, hdc in top of beg ch-2, turn.

Row 70: Ch 2, work 21 sts, with CC2 work 2 sts, with CC work 18 sts, with CC2 work 1 st, with MC work 18 sts, hdc in top of beg ch-2, turn.

Row 71: Ch 2, work 17 sts, with CC2 work 2 sts, with CC work 18 sts, with CC2 work 2 sts, with MC work 21 sts, hdc in top of beg ch-2, turn.

Row 72: Ch 2, work 21 sts, with CC2 work 2 sts, with CC work 18 sts, with CC2 work 2 sts, with MC work 17 sts, hdc in top of beg ch-2, turn.

Row 73: Ch 2, work 17 sts, with CC2 work 2 sts, with CC work 19 sts, with CC2 work 1 st, with MC work 21 sts, hdc in top of beg ch-2, turn.

Row 74: Ch 2, work 21 sts, with CC2 work 1 st, with CC work 20 sts, with CC2 work 1 st, with MC work 17 sts, hdc in top of beg ch-2, turn.

Row 75: Ch 2, work 17 sts, with CC2 work 1 st, with CC work 20 sts, with CC2 work 1 st, with MC work 21 sts, hdc in top of beg ch-2, turn.

Row 76: Ch 2, work 21 sts, with CC2 work 1 st, with CC work 20 sts, with CC2 work 1 st, with MC work 17 sts, hdc in top of beg ch-2, turn.

Row 77: Ch 2, work 17 sts, with CC2 work 1 st, with CC work 20 sts, with CC2 work 1 st, with MC work 21 sts, hdc in top of beg ch-2, turn.

Row 78: Ch 2, work 20 sts, with CC2 work 2 sts, with CC work 20 sts, with CC2 work 1 st, with MC work 5 sts, with CC2 work 2 sts, with MC work 10 sts, hdc in top of beg ch-2, turn.

Row 79: Ch 2, work 9 sts, with CC2 work 4 sts, with MC work 4 sts, with CC2 work 1 st, with CC work 20 sts, with CC2 work 2 sts, with MC work 20 sts, hdc in top of beg ch-2, turn.

Row 80: Ch 2, work 20 sts, with CC2 work 2 sts, with CC work 20 sts, with CC2 work 1 st, with MC work 3 sts, with CC2 work 2 sts, with CC work 2 sts, with CC2 work 1 st, with MC work 9 sts, hdc in top of beg ch-2, turn.

Row 81: Ch 2, work 9 sts, with CC2 work 1 st, with CC work 3 sts, with CC2 work 1 st, with MC work 3 sts, with CC2 work 1 st, with CC work 20 sts, with CC2 work 2 sts, with MC work 20 sts, hdc in top of beg ch-2, turn.

Row 82: Ch 2, work 20 sts, with CC2 work 2 sts, with CC work 20 sts, with CC2 work 1 st, with MC work 2 sts, with CC2 work 2 sts, with CC work 3 sts, with CC2 work 1 st, with MC work 9 sts, hdc in top of beg ch-2, turn.

Row 83: Ch 2, work 9 sts, with CC2 work 1 st, with CC work 4 sts, with CC2 work 1 st, with MC work 2 sts, with CC2 work 1 st, with CC work 21 sts, with CC2 work 1 st, with MC work 20 sts, hdc in top of beg ch-2, turn.

Row 84: Ch 2, work 20 sts, with CC2 work 1 st, with CC work 21 sts, with CC2 work 1 st, with MC work 1 st, with CC2 work 2 sts, with CC work 3 sts, with CC2 work 2 sts, with MC work 9 sts, hdc in top of beg ch-2, turn.

Row 85: Ch 2, work 10 sts, with CC2 work 2 sts, with CC work 3 sts, with CC2 work 1 st, with MC work 1 st, with CC2 work 1 st, with CC work 21 sts, with CC2 work 1 st, with MC work 20 sts, hdc in top of beg ch-2, turn.

Row 86: Ch 2, work 20 sts, with CC2 work 1 st, with CC work 21 sts, with CC2 work 3 sts, with CC work 3 sts, with CC2 work 2 sts, with MC work 10 sts, hdc in top of beg ch-2, turn.

Row 87: Ch 2, work 11 sts, with CC2 work 1 st, with CC work 3 sts, with CC2 work 3 sts, with CC work 21 sts, with CC2 work 1 st, with MC work 20 sts, hdc in top of beg ch-2, turn.

Row 88: Ch 2, work 20 sts, with CC2 work 1 st, with CC work 20 sts, with CC2 work 3 sts, with CC work 3 sts, with CC2 work 2 sts, with MC work 11 sts, hdc in top of beg ch-2, turn.

Row 89: Ch 2, work 11 sts, with CC2 work 2 sts, with CC work 4 sts, with CC2 work 2 sts, with CC work 20 sts, with CC2 work 1 st, with MC work 20 sts, hdc in top of beg ch-2, turn.

Row 90: Ch 2, work 18 sts, with CC2 work 3 sts, with CC work 20 sts, with CC2 work 1 st, with CC work 5 sts, with CC2 work 1 st, with MC work 12 sts, hdc in top of beg ch-2, turn.

Row 91: Ch 2, work 12 sts, with CC2 work 1 st, with CC work 27 sts, with CC2 work 2 sts, with MC work 18 sts, hdc in top of beg ch-2, turn.

Row 92: Ch 2, work 17 sts, with CC2 work 2 sts, with CC work 28 sts, with CC2 work 1 st, with MC work 12 sts, hdc in top of beg ch-2, turn.

Row 93: Ch 2, work 12 sts, with CC2 work 2 sts, with CC work 28 sts, with CC2 work 3 sts, with MC work 15 sts, hdc in top of beg ch-2, turn.

Row 94: Ch 2, work 14 sts, with CC2 work 3 sts, with CC work 28 sts, with CC2 work 2 sts, with MC work 13 sts, hdc in top of beg ch-2, turn.

Row 95: Ch 2, work 14 sts, with CC2 work 1 st, with CC work 30 sts, with CC2 work 3 sts, with MC work 12 sts, hdc in top of beg ch-2, turn.

Row 96: Ch 2, work 10 sts, with CC2 work 4 sts, with CC work 31 sts, with CC2 work 1 st, with MC work 14 sts, hdc in top of beg ch-2, turn.

Row 97: Ch 2, work 14 sts, with CC2 work 2 sts, with CC work 32 sts, with CC2 work 4 sts, with MC work 8 sts, hdc in top of beg ch-2, turn.

Row 98: Ch 2, work 8 sts, with CC2 work 1 st, with CC work 34 sts, with CC2 work 3 sts, with MC work 14 sts, hdc in top of beg ch-2, turn.

Row 99: Ch 2, work 15 sts, with CC2 work 2 sts, with CC work 33 sts, with CC2 work 2 sts, with MC work 8 sts, hdc in top of beg ch-2, turn.

Row 100: Ch 2, work 9 sts, with CC2 work 2 sts, with CC work 32 sts, with CC2 work 1 st, with MC work 16 sts, hdc in top of beg ch-2, turn.

Row 101: Ch 2, work 15 sts, with CC2 work 2 sts, with CC work 32 sts, with CC2 work 1 st, with MC work 10 sts, hdc in top of beg ch-2, turn.

Row 102: Ch 2, work 10 sts, with CC2 work 2 sts, with CC work 31 sts, with CC2 work 2 sts, with MC work 15 sts, hdc in top of beg ch-2, turn.

Row 103: Ch 2, work 15 sts, with CC2 work 1 st, with CC work 31 sts, with CC2 work 2 sts, with MC work 11 sts, hdc in top of beg ch-2, turn.

Row 104: Ch 2, work 12 sts, with CC2 work 1 st, with CC work 31 sts, with CC2 work 1 st, with MC work 15 sts, hdc in top of beg ch-2, turn.

Row 105: Ch 2, work 15 sts, with CC2 work 1 st, with CC work 30 sts, with CC2 work 2 sts, with MC work 12 sts, hdc in top of beg ch-2, turn.

Row 106: Ch 2, work 13 sts, with CC2 work 2 sts, with CC work 29 sts, with CC2 work 1 st, with MC work 15 sts, hdc in top of beg ch-2, turn.

Row 107: Ch 2, work 15 sts, with CC2 work 1 st, with CC work 28 sts, with CC2 work 2 sts, with MC work 14 sts, hdc in top of beg ch-2, turn.

Row 108: Ch 2, work 15 sts, with CC2 work 2 sts, with CC work 27 sts, with CC2 work 1 st, with MC work 15 sts, hdc in top of beg ch-2, turn.

Row 109: Ch 2, work 15 sts, with CC2 work 1 st, with CC work 24 sts, with CC2 work 4 sts, with MC work 16 sts, hdc in top of beg ch-2, turn.

Row 110: Ch 2, work 17 sts, with CC2 work 4 sts, with CC work 22 sts, with CC2 work 2 sts, with MC work 15 sts, hdc in top of beg ch-2, turn.

Row 111: Ch 2, work 15 sts, with CC2 work 2 sts, with CC work 21 sts, with CC2 work 3 sts, with MC work 19 sts, hdc in top of beg ch-2, turn.

Row 112: Ch 2, work 20 sts, with CC2 work 2 sts, with CC work 21 sts, with CC2 work 2 sts, with MC work 15 sts, hdc in top of beg ch-2, turn.

Row 113: Ch 2, work 15 sts, with CC2 work 2 sts, with CC work 21 sts, with CC2 work 1 st, with MC work 21 sts, hdc in top of beg ch-2, turn.

Row 114: Ch 2, work 21 sts, with CC2 work 1 st, with CC work 21 sts, with CC2 work 1 st, with MC work 16 sts, hdc in top of beg ch-2, turn.

Row 115: Ch 2, work 16 sts, with CC2 work 1 st, with CC work 20 sts, with CC2 work 2 sts, with MC work 21 sts, hdc in top of beg ch-2, turn.

Row 116: Ch 2, work 21 sts, with CC2 work 2 sts, with CC work 20 sts, with CC2 work 1 st, with MC work 16 sts, hdc in top of beg ch-2, turn.

Row 117: Ch 2, work 16 sts, with CC2 work 2 sts, with CC work 19 sts, with CC2 work 1 st, with MC work 22 sts, hdc in top of beg ch-2, turn.

Row 118: Ch 2, work 22 sts, with CC2 work 2 sts, with CC work 18 sts, with CC2 work 2 sts, with MC work 16 sts, hdc in top of beg ch-2, turn.

Row 119: Ch 2, work 16 sts, with CC2 work 2 sts, with CC work 18 sts, with CC2 work 2 sts, with MC work 22 sts, hdc in top of beg ch-2, turn.

Row 120: Ch 2, work 23 sts, with CC2 work 1 st, with CC work 18 sts, with CC2 work 2 sts, with MC work 16 sts, hdc in to of beg ch-2, turn.

Row 121: Ch 2, work 17 sts, with CC2 work 1 st, with CC work 17 sts, with CC2 work 2 sts, with MC work 23 sts, hdc in top of beg ch-2, turn.

Row 122: Ch 2, work 23 sts, with CC2 work 2 sts, with CC work 17 sts, with CC2 work 1 st, with MC work 17 sts, hdc in top of beg ch-2, turn.

Row 123: Ch 2, work 17 sts, with CC2 work 1 st, with CC work 17 sts, with CC2 work 1 st, with MC work 24 sts, hdc in top of beg ch-2, turn.

Row 124: Ch 2, work 24 sts, with CC2 work 2 sts, with CC work 15 sts, with CC2 work 2 sts, with MC work 17 sts, hdc in top of beg ch-2, turn.

Row 125: Ch 2, work 17 sts, with CC2 work 2 sts, with CC work 15 sts, with CC2 work 2 sts, with MC work 24 sts, hdc in top of beg ch-2.

Fasten off all colors.

Border

Note: *Blanket is reversible up to this point. Decide which side you like as the front and make sure right side is facing you as you complete the blanket border.*

Rnd 1 (RS): Hold blanket with RS facing and foundation ch at top, join CC2 in first ch in right-hand corner, ch 1, 3 sc in first ch, sc in each ch across to last ch, 3 sc in last ch, rotate blanket to work in row ends, work 3 sc for every 2 rows across side, rotate blanket to work across top row, 3 sc in first st, sc in each st across to last st, 3 sc in last st, rotate blanket to work in row ends, work 3 sc for every 2 rows across side, join in top of first sc. Fasten off. *(126 sts along top and bottom, 188 sts along each side; 628 sts around blanket)*

Twisting Border
Work same as Twisting Border on page 5. ●

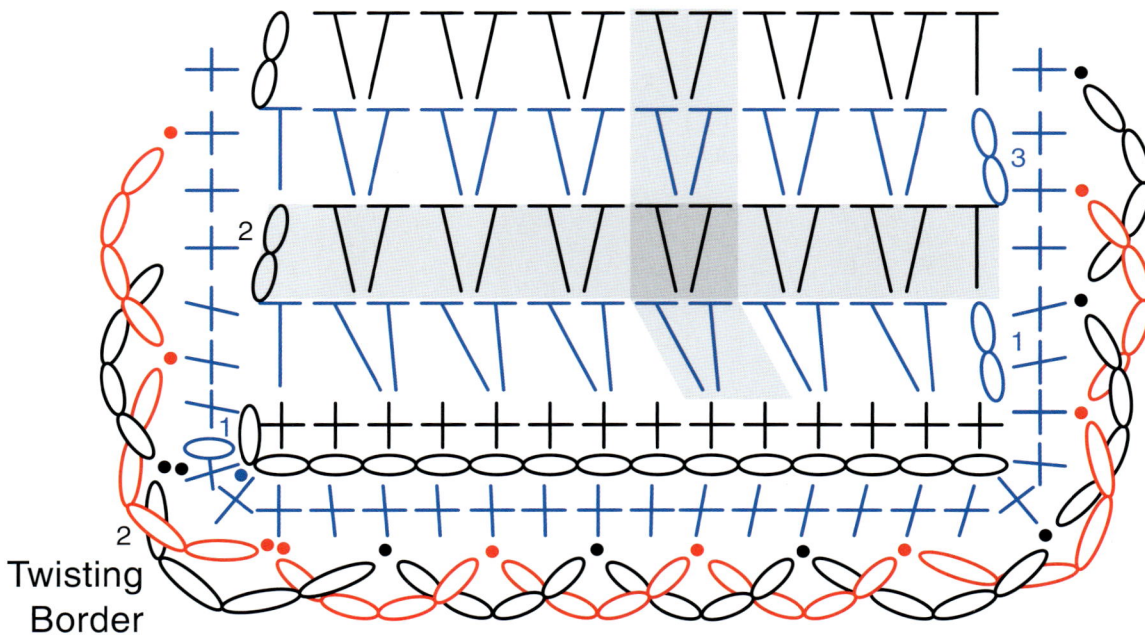

Shark Bait
Reduced Sample of Stitch Diagram
Note: Rep shown in gray.

STITCH KEY

⬯	Chain (ch)
•	Slip stitch (sl st)
+	Single crochet (sc)
T	Half double crochet (hdc)
V	Mini V-stitch (mini V-st)

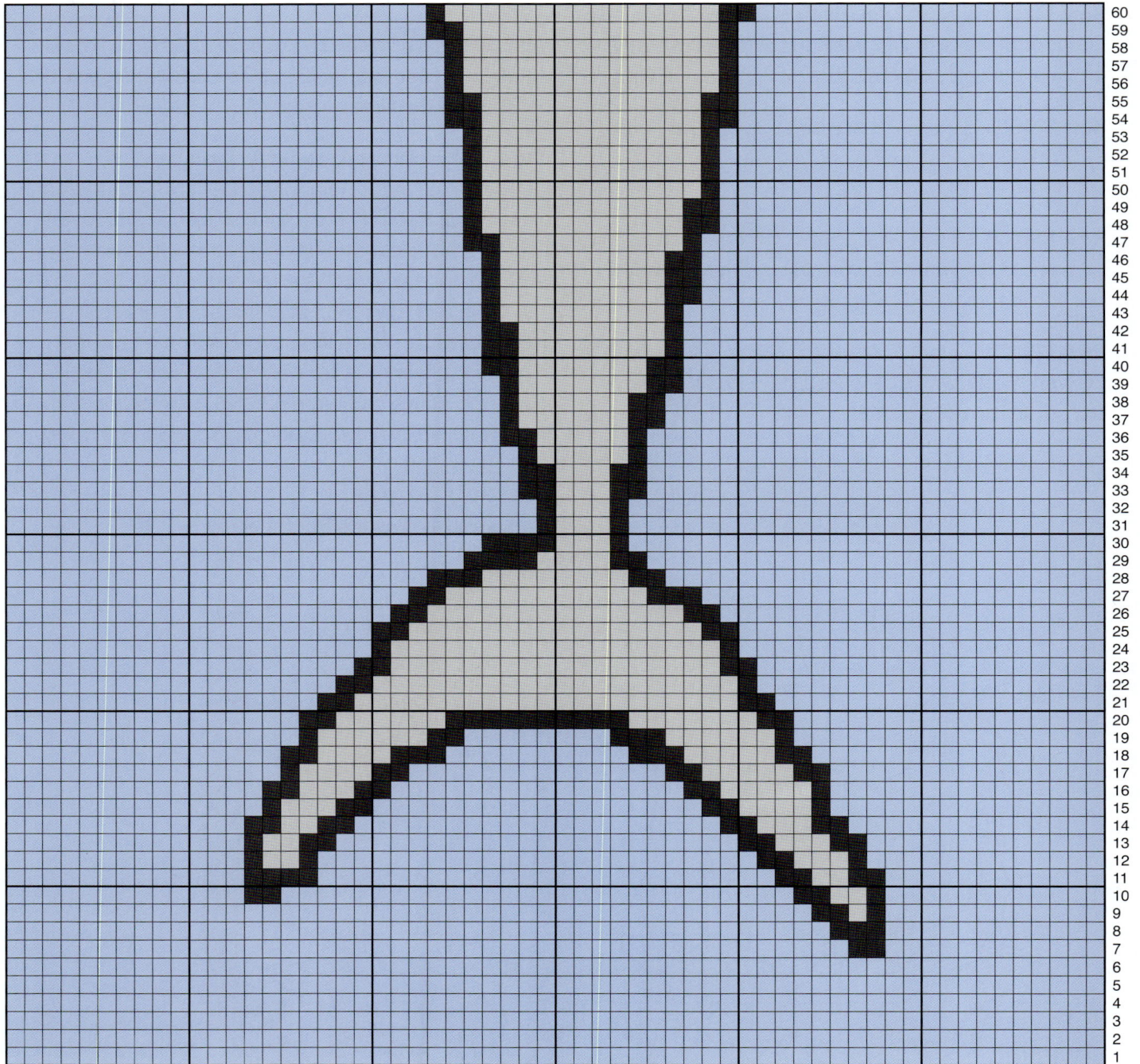

Shark Bait
Chart (A)

COLOR KEY
- Contrasting Color - Silhouette
- Contrasting Color 2 - Outline
- Main Color - Background

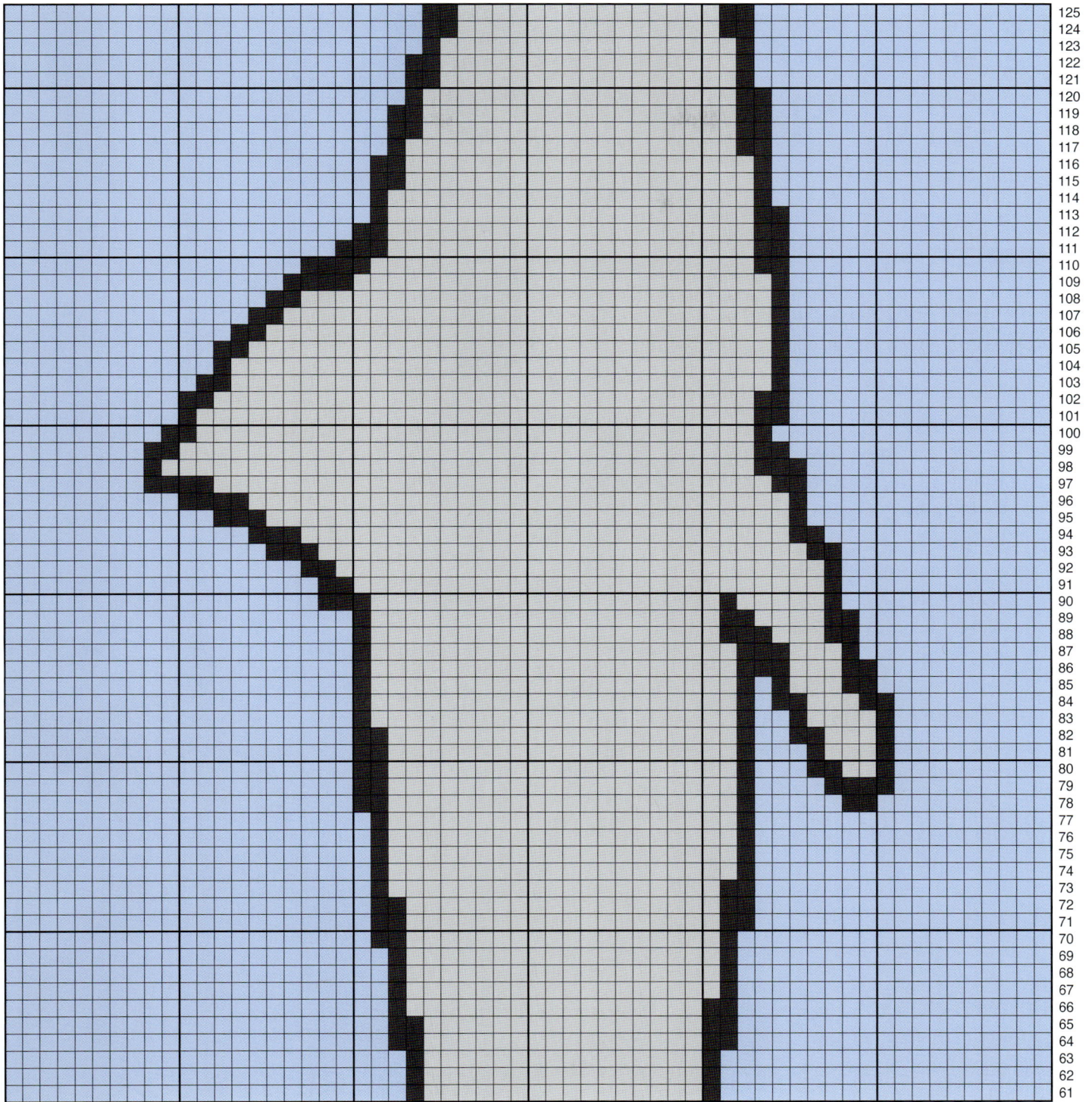

Shark Bait
Chart (B)

You Octopi My Heart

Skill Level

◼◼◻◻ EASY

Finished Measurements

Approximately 38 inches wide x 48 inches long

Materials

- Red Heart Super Saver Ombré medium (worsted) weight acrylic yarn (10 oz/482 yds/283g per skein):
    - 3 skeins #3969 violet (MC)
- Red Heart Super Saver medium (worsted) weight acrylic yarn (7 oz/364 yds/198g per skein):
    - 2 skeins #505 Aruba sea (CC)
    - 1 skein #311 white (CC2)
- Size I/9/5.5mm crochet hook or size needed to obtain gauge
- Tapestry needle
- Bobbins (optional)

4 MEDIUM

Gauge

11 sts = 4 inches; 15 rows = 4 inches

Pattern Notes

Before beginning, we suggest you read the General Instructions on pages 2–6 for information needed to work the pattern.

Refer to Stitch Diagrams and Color Chart as needed.

All rows begin with MC.

Weave in loose ends as work progresses.

Chain-2 at beginning of row counts as a half double crochet unless otherwise stated.

Special Stitch

Mini V-stitch (mini V-st): 2 hdc in indicated st or sp.

Afghan

Foundation row (WS): With MC, ch 123, sc in 2nd ch from hook and in each rem sc across, turn. *(122 sts)*

Row 1 (RS): Ch 2 *(see Pattern Notes),* **mini V-st** *(see Special Stitch)* in next st, sk next st, rep from * across to last st, hdc in last st, turn. *(60 sts, 2 hdc)*

Row 2: Ch 2, *mini V-st in between hdc of each mini V-st across, hdc in top of beg ch-2, turn.

Rows 3–13: Rep row 2.

Row 14: Ch 2, mini V-st in each of next 38 sts, **changing color** *(see General Instructions)* to CC2 in last leg of last mini V-st, mini V-st between hdc of each of next 3 mini V-sts, changing color to MC in last leg of last mini V-st, mini V-st between hdc of each of next 19 mini V-sts, hdc in top of beg ch-2, turn.

Note: On following rows, mini V-sts will be referred to as sts.

Row 15: Ch 2, work 19 sts, with CC2 work 1 st, with CC work 1 st, with CC2 work 1 st, with MC work 38 sts, hdc in top of beg ch-2, turn.

Row 16: Ch 2, work 37 sts, with CC2 work 2 sts, with CC work 2 sts, with CC2 work 1 st, with MC work 18 sts, hdc in top of beg ch-2, turn.

Row 17: Ch 2, work 18 sts, with CC2 work 1 st, with CC work 3 sts, with CC2 work 1 st, with MC work 37 sts, hdc in top of beg ch-2, turn.

Row 18: Ch 2, work 22 sts, with CC2 work 2 sts, with MC work 13 sts, with CC2 work 1 st, with CC work 3 sts, with CC2 work 1 st, with MC work 18 sts, hdc in top of beg ch-2, turn.

Row 19: Ch 2, work 18 sts, with CC2 work 1 st, with CC work 3 sts, with CC2 work 1 st, with MC work 12 sts, with CC2 work 4 sts, with MC work 21 sts, hdc in top of beg ch-2, turn.

Row 20: Ch 2, work 21 sts, with CC2 work 1 st, with CC work 2 sts, with CC2 work 2 sts, with MC work 10 sts, with CC2 work 2 sts, with CC work 2 sts, with CC2 work 1 st, with MC work 19 sts, hdc in top of beg ch-2, turn.

Row 21: Ch 2, work 19 sts, with CC2 work 2 sts, with CC work 2 sts, with CC2 work 1 st, with MC work 10 sts, with CC2 work 1 st, with CC work 3 sts, with CC2 work 1 st, with MC work 21 sts, hdc in top of beg ch-2, turn.

Row 22: Ch 2, work 21 sts, with CC2 work 2 sts, with CC work 2 sts, with CC2 work 1 st, with MC work 10 sts, with CC2 work 1 st, with CC work 2 sts, with CC2 work 1 st, with MC work 20 sts, hdc in top of beg ch-2, turn.

Row 23: Ch 2, work 20 sts, with CC2 work 1 st, with CC work 2 sts, with CC2 work 1 st, with MC work 9 sts, with CC2 work 1 st, with CC work 2 sts, with CC2 work 2 sts, with MC work 22 sts, hdc in top of beg ch-2, turn.

Row 24: Ch 2, work 23 sts, with CC2 work 1 st, with CC work 2 sts, with CC2 work 1 st, with MC work 9 sts, with CC2 work 1 st, with CC work 2 sts, with CC2 work 1 st, with MC work 20 sts, hdc in top of beg ch-2, turn.

Row 25: Ch 2, work 20 sts, with CC2 work 1 st, with CC work 3 sts, with CC2 work 1 st, with MC work 8 sts, with CC2 work 1 st, with CC work 2 sts, with CC2 work 1 st, with MC work 23 sts, hdc in top of beg ch-2, turn.

Row 26: Ch 2, work 23 sts, with CC2 work 1 st, with CC work 2 sts, with CC2 work 1 st, with MC work 8 sts, with CC2 work 1 st, with CC work 3 sts, with CC2 work 1 st, with MC work 20 sts, hdc in top of beg ch-2, turn.

Row 27: Ch 2, work 20 sts, with CC2 work 2 sts, with CC work 2 sts, with CC2 work 1 st, with MC work 8 sts, with CC2 work 1 st, with CC work 2 sts, with CC2 work 1 st, with MC work 23 sts, hdc in top of beg ch-2, turn.

Row 28: Ch 2, work 23 sts, with CC2 work 1 st, with CC work 2 sts, with CC2 work 1 st, with MC work 8 sts, with CC2 work 1 st, with CC work 2 sts, with CC2 work 1 st, with MC work 21 sts, hdc in top of beg ch-2, turn.

Row 29: Ch 2, work 21 sts, with CC2 work 1 st, with CC work 2 sts, with CC2 work 2 sts, with MC work 7 sts, with CC2 work 1 st, with CC work 2 sts, with CC2 work 1 st, with MC work 8 sts, with CC2 work 1 st, with MC work 14 sts, hdc in top of beg ch-2, turn.

Row 30: Ch 2, work 13 sts, with CC2 work 3 sts, with MC work 7 sts, with CC2 work 1 st, with CC work 2 sts, with CC2 work 1 st, with MC work 7 sts, with CC2 work 1 st, with CC work 2 sts, with CC2 work 2 sts, with MC work 21 sts, hdc in top of beg ch-2, turn.

Row 31: Ch 2, work 6 sts, with CC2 work 2 sts, with MC work 13 sts, with CC2 work 2 sts, with CC work 2 sts, with CC2 work 1 st, with MC work 7 sts, with CC2 work 1 st, with CC work 2 sts, with CC2 work 1 st, with MC work 7 sts, with CC2 work 1 st, with CC work 1 st, with CC2 work 1 st, with MC work 13 sts, hdc in top of beg ch-2, turn.

Row 32: Ch 2, work 13 sts, with CC2 work 1 st, with CC work 1 st, with CC2 work 2 sts, with MC work 5 sts, with CC2 work 2 sts, with CC work 2 sts, with CC2 work 1 st, with MC work 6 sts, with CC2 work 2 sts, with CC work 2 sts, with CC2 work 2 sts, with MC work 12 sts, with CC2 work 4 sts, with MC work 5 sts, hdc in top of beg ch-2, turn.

Row 33: Ch 2, work 5 sts, with CC2 work 1 st, with CC work 2 sts, with CC2 work 2 sts, with MC work 12 sts, with CC2 work 2 sts, with CC work 2 sts, with CC2 work 1 st, with MC work 6 sts, with CC2 work 1 st, with CC work 3 sts, with CC2 work 1 st, with MC work 5 sts, with CC2 work 1 st, with CC work 2 sts, with CC2 work 1 st, with MC work 13 sts, hdc in top of beg ch-2, turn.

Row 34: Ch 2, work 13 sts, with CC2 work 1 st, with CC work 2 sts, with CC2 work 1 st, with MC work 5 sts, with CC2 work 1 st, with CC work 3 sts, with CC2 work 1 st, with MC work 6 sts, with CC2 work 1 st, with CC work 2 sts, with CC2 work 1 st, with MC work 13 sts, with CC2 work 1 st, with CC work 3 sts, with CC2 work 1 st, with MC work 5 sts, hdc in top of beg ch-2, turn.

Row 35: Ch 2, work 5 sts, with CC2 work 1 st, with CC work 3 sts, with CC2 work 2 sts, with MC work 12 sts, with CC2 work 1 st, with CC work 2 sts, with CC2 work 2 sts, with MC work 6 sts, with CC2 work 1 st, with CC work 2 sts, with CC2 work 2 sts, with MC work 4 sts, with CC2 work 1 st, with CC work 2 sts, with CC2 work 1 st, with MC work 13 sts, hdc in top of beg ch-2, turn.

Row 36: Ch 2, work 12 sts, with CC2 work 2 sts, with CC work 2 sts, with CC2 work 1 st, with MC work 4 sts, with CC2 work 1 st, with CC work 3 sts, with CC2 work 1 st, with MC work 6 sts, with CC2 work 1 st, with CC work 3 sts, with CC2 work 1 st, with MC work 12 sts, with CC2 work 1 st, with CC work 3 sts, with CC2 work 2 sts, with MC work 5 sts, hdc in top of beg ch-2, turn.

Row 37: Ch 2, work 6 sts, with CC2 work 1 st, with CC work 3 sts, with CC2 work 1 st, with MC work 12 sts, with CC2 work 1 st, with CC work 3 sts, with CC2 work 1 st, with MC work 6 sts, with CC2 work 1 st, with CC work 3 sts, with CC2 work 1 st, with MC work 4 sts, with CC2 work 1 st, with CC work 3 sts, with CC2 work 1 st, with MC work 12 sts, hdc in top of beg ch-2, turn.

Row 38: Ch 2, work 11 sts, with CC2 work 2 sts, with CC work 2 sts, with CC2 work 2 sts, with MC work 3 sts, with CC2 work 2 sts, with CC work 3 sts, with CC2 work 1 st, with MC work 6 sts, with CC2 work 1 st, with CC work 3 sts, with CC2 work 2 sts, with MC work 10 sts, with CC2 work 2 sts, with CC work 2 sts, with CC2 work 2 sts, with MC work 6 sts, hdc in top of beg ch-2, turn.

Row 39: Ch 2, work 7 sts, with CC2 work 1 st, with CC work 3 sts, with CC2 work 1 st, with MC work 10 sts, with CC2 work 1 st, with CC work 4 sts, with CC2 work 1 st, with MC work 6 sts, with CC2 work 2 sts, with CC work 3 sts, with CC2 work 1 st, with MC work 4 sts, with CC2 work 2 sts, with CC work 2 sts, with CC2 work 1 st, with MC work 11 sts, hdc in top of beg ch-2, turn.

Row 40: Ch 2, work 10 sts, with CC2 work 2 sts, with CC work 2 sts, with CC2 work 1 st, with MC work 4 sts, with CC2 work 2 sts, with CC work 2 sts, with CC2 work 2 sts, with MC work 7 sts, with CC2 work 2 sts, with CC work 3 sts, with CC2 work 1 st, with MC work 10 sts, with CC2 work 1 st, with CC work 3 sts, with CC2 work 1 st, with MC work 7 sts, hdc in top of beg ch-2, turn.

Row 41: Ch 2, work 7 sts, with CC2 work 2 sts, with CC work 2 sts, with CC2 work 2 sts, with MC work 9 sts, with CC2 work 1 st, with CC work 3 sts, with CC2 work 1 st, with MC work 9 sts, with CC2 work 1 st, with CC work 2 sts, with CC2 work 2 sts, with MC work 4 sts, with CC2 work 1 st, with CC work 3 sts, with CC2 work 1 st, with MC work 10 sts, hdc in top of beg ch-2, turn.

Row 42: Ch 2, work 10 sts, with CC2 work 1 st, with CC work 2 sts, with CC2 work 2 sts, with MC work 4 sts, with CC2 work 1 st, with CC work 3 sts, with CC2 work 1 st, with MC work 9 sts, with CC2 work 1 st, with CC work 3 sts, with CC2 work 2 sts, with MC work 8 sts, with CC2 work 1 st, with CC work 3 sts, with CC2 work 1 st, with MC work 8 sts, hdc in top of beg ch-2, turn.

Row 43: Ch 2, work 8 sts, with CC2 work 1 st, with CC work 3 sts, with CC2 work 2 sts, with MC work 7 sts, with CC2 work 1 st, with CC work 4 sts, with CC2 work 1 st, with MC work 9 sts, with CC2 work 1 st, with CC work 3 sts, with CC2 work 1 st, with MC work 5 sts, with CC2 work 1 st, with CC work 2 sts, with CC2 work 2 sts, with MC work 9 sts, hdc in top of beg ch-2, turn.

Row 44: Ch 2, work 9 sts, with CC2 work 1 st, with CC work 2 sts, with CC2 work 2 sts, with MC work 5 sts, with CC2 work 1 st, with CC work 3 sts, with CC2 work 1 st, with MC work 10 sts, with CC2 work 1 st, with CC work 3 sts, with CC2 work 1 st, with MC work 7 sts, with CC2 work 1 st, with CC work 3 sts, with CC2 work 2 sts, with MC work 8 sts, hdc in top of beg ch-2, turn.

Row 45: Ch 2, work 9 sts, with CC2 work 1 st, with CC work 3 sts, with CC2 work 2 sts, with MC work 6 sts, with CC2 work 1 st, with CC work 3 sts, with CC2 work 1 st, with MC work 10 sts, with CC2 work 1 st, with CC work 3 sts, with CC2 work 1 st, with MC work 6 sts, with CC2 work 1 st, with CC work 2 sts, with CC2 work 2 sts, with MC work 8 sts, hdc in top of beg ch-2, turn.

Row 46: Ch 2, work 8 sts, with CC2 work 1 st, with CC work 3 sts, with CC2 work 1 st, with MC work 6 sts, with CC2 work 1 st, with CC work 3 sts, with CC2 work 2 sts, with MC work 9 sts, with CC2 work 1 st, with CC work 3 sts, with CC2 work 1 st, with MC work 5 sts, with CC2 work 2 sts, with CC work 4 sts, with CC2 work 1 st, with MC work 9 sts, hdc in top of beg ch-2, turn.

Row 47: Ch 2, work 2 sts, with CC2 work 2 sts, with MC work 6 sts, with CC2 work 1 st, with CC work 4 sts, with CC2 work 1 st, with MC work 5 sts, with CC2 work 1 st, with CC work 3 sts, with CC2 work 1 st, with MC work 9 sts, with CC2 work 2 sts, with CC work 3 sts, with CC2 work 1 st, with MC work 6 sts, with CC2 work 2 sts, with CC work 2 sts, with CC2 work 2 sts, with MC work 7 sts, hdc in top of beg ch-2, turn.

Row 48: Ch 2, work 7 sts, with CC2 work 1 st, with CC work 3 sts, with CC2 work 1 st, with MC work 7 sts, with CC2 work 1 st, with CC work 4 sts, with CC2 work 1 st, with MC work 9 sts, with CC2 work 1 st, with CC work 3 sts, with CC2 work 2 sts, with MC work 3 sts, with CC2 work 2 sts, with CC work 3 sts, with CC2 work 2 sts, with MC work 5 sts, with CC2 work 4 sts, with MC work 1 st, hdc in top of beg ch-2, turn.

Row 49: Ch 2, work 1 st, with CC2 work 1 st, with CC work 2 sts, with CC2 work 1 st, with MC work 6 sts, with CC2 work 1 st, with CC work 4 sts, with CC2 work 1 st, with MC work 3 sts, with CC2 work 2 sts, with CC work 3 sts, with CC2 work 1 st, with MC work 9 sts, with CC2 work 1 st, with CC work 3 sts, with CC2 work 2 sts, with MC work 7 sts, with CC2 work 1 st, with CC work 3 sts, with CC2 work 1 st, with MC work 7 sts, hdc in top of beg ch-2, turn.

Row 50: Ch 2, work 7 sts, with CC2 work 1 st, with CC work 3 sts, with CC2 work 1 st, with MC work 8 sts, with CC2 work 1 st, with CC work 3 sts, with CC2 work 2 sts, with MC work 8 sts, with CC2 work 2 sts, with CC work 3 sts, with CC2 work 1 st, with MC work 3 sts, with CC2 work 1 st, with CC work 4 sts, with CC2 work

1 st, with MC work 5 sts, with CC2 work 2 sts, with CC work 2 sts, with CC2 work 1 st, with MC work 1 st, hdc in top of beg ch-2, turn.

Row 51: Ch 2, work 1 st, with CC2 work 2 sts, with CC work 2 sts, with CC2 work 2 sts, with MC work 4 sts, with CC2 work 1 st, with CC work 4 sts, with CC2 work 1 st, with MC work 3 sts, with CC2 work 1 st, with CC work 3 sts, with CC2 work 1 st, with MC work 9 sts, with CC2 work 1 st, with CC work 4 sts, with CC2 work 1 st, with MC work 8 sts, with CC2 work 1 st, with CC work 3 sts, with CC2 work 1 st, with MC work 7 sts, hdc in top of beg ch-2, turn.

Row 52: Ch 2, work 7 sts, with CC2 work 1 st, with CC work 3 sts, with CC2 work 1 st, with MC work 8 sts, with CC2 work 1 st, with CC work 5 sts, with CC2 work 1 st, with MC work 8 sts, with CC2 work 1 st, with CC work 3 sts, with CC2 work 1 st, with MC work 2 sts, with CC2 work 2 sts, with CC work 3 sts, with CC2 work 2 sts, with MC work 4 sts, with CC2 work 1 st, with CC work 3 sts, with CC2 work 1 st, with MC work 2 sts, hdc in top of beg ch-2, turn.

Row 53: Ch 2, work 2 sts, with CC2 work 2 sts, with CC work 2 sts, with CC2 work 1 st, with MC work 5 sts, with CC2 work 1 st, with CC work 4 sts, with CC2 work 1 st, with MC work 2 sts, with CC2 work 1 st, with CC work 3 sts, with CC2 work 1 st, with MC work 8 sts, with CC2 work 1 st, with CC work 4 sts, with CC2 work 2 sts, with MC work 8 sts, with CC2 work 1 st, with CC work 3 sts, with CC2 work 1 st, with MC work 7 sts, hdc in top of beg ch-2, turn.

Row 54: Ch 2, work 7 sts, with CC2 work 1 st, with CC work 3 sts, with CC2 work 1 st, with MC work 9 sts, with CC2 work 1 st, with CC work 4 sts, with CC2 work 2 sts, with MC work 7 sts, with CC2 work 1 st, with CC work 3 sts, with CC2 work 1 st, with MC work 2 sts, with CC2 work 1 st, with CC work 4 sts, with CC2 work 1 st, with MC work 5 sts, with CC2 work 1 st, with CC work 2 sts, with CC2 work 1 st, with MC work 3 sts, hdc in top of beg ch-2, turn.

Row 55: Ch 2, work 3 sts, with CC2 work 1 st, with CC work 2 sts, with CC2 work 1 st, with MC work 5 sts, with CC2 work 1 st, with CC work 4 sts, with CC2 work 1 st, with MC work 2 sts, with CC2 work 1 st, with CC work 3 sts, with CC2 work 1 st, with MC work 7 sts, with CC2 work 1 st, with CC work 4 sts, with CC2 work 2 sts, with MC work 8 sts, with CC2 work 2 sts, with CC work 3 sts, with CC2 work 1 st, with MC work 7 sts, hdc in top of beg ch-2, turn.

Row 56: Ch 2, work 7 sts, with CC2 work 1 st, with CC work 4 sts, with CC2 work 1 st, with MC work 9 sts, with CC2 work 1 st, with CC work 4 sts, with CC2 work 2 sts, with MC work 6 sts, with CC2 work 1 st, with CC work 3 sts, with CC2 work 1 st, with MC work 2 sts, with CC2 work 1 st, with CC work 3 sts, with CC2 work 2 sts, with MC work 5 sts, with CC2 work 1 st, with CC work 2 sts, with CC2 work 1 st, with MC work 3 sts, hdc in top of beg ch-2, turn.

Row 57: Ch 2, work 3 sts, with CC2 work 1 st, with CC work 2 sts, with CC2 work 1 st, with MC work 6 sts, with CC2 work 1 st, with CC work 3 sts, with CC2 work 1 st, with MC work 2 sts, with CC2 work 1 st, with CC work 3 sts, with CC2 work 1 st, with MC work 6 sts, with CC2 work 1 st, with CC work 5 sts, with CC2 work 1 st, with MC work 9 sts, with CC2 work 1 st, with CC work 3 sts, with CC2 work 2 sts, with MC work 7 sts, hdc in top of beg ch-2, turn.

Row 58: Ch 2, work 8 sts, with CC2 work 1 st, with CC work 3 sts, with CC2 work 1 st, with MC work 9 sts, with CC2 work 2 sts, with CC work 4 sts, with CC2 work 1 st, with MC work 6 sts, with CC2 work 1 st, with CC work 3 sts, with CC2 work 1 st, with MC work 2 sts, with CC2 work 1 st, with CC work 3 sts, with CC2 work 1 st, with MC work 6 sts, with CC2 work 2 sts, with CC work 2 sts, with CC2 work 1 st, with MC work 2 sts, hdc in top of beg ch-2, turn.

Row 59: Ch 2, work 2 sts, with CC2 work 1 st, with CC work 2 sts, with CC2 work 1 st, with MC work 7 sts, with CC2 work 1 st, with CC work 3 sts, with CC2 work 1 st, with MC work 2 sts, with CC2 work 1 st, with CC work 3 sts, with CC2 work 1 st, with MC work 5 sts, with CC2 work 2 sts, with CC work 4 sts, with CC2 work 1 st, with MC work 9 sts, with CC2 work 2 sts, with CC work 3 sts, with CC2 work 1 st, with MC work 8 sts, hdc in top of beg ch-2, turn.

Row 60: Ch 2, work 8 sts, with CC2 work 1 st, with CC work 4 sts, with CC2 work 1 st, with MC work 9 sts, with CC2 work 2 sts, with CC work 4 sts, with CC2 work 1 st, with MC work 5 sts, with CC2 work 1 st, with CC work 3 sts, with CC2 work 1 st, with MC work 2 sts, with CC2 work 1 st, with CC work 3 sts, with CC2 work 1 st, with MC work 7 sts, with CC2 work 1 st, with CC work 2 sts, with CC2 work 1 st, with MC work 2 sts, hdc in top of beg ch-2, turn.

Row 61: Ch 2, work 2 sts, with CC2 work 1 st, with CC work 2 sts, with CC2 work 1 st, with MC work 7 sts, with CC2 work 1 st, with CC work 3 sts, with CC2 work 1 st, with MC work 2 sts, with CC2 work 1 st, with CC work 3 sts, with CC2 work 1 st, with MC work 4 sts, with CC2 work 2 sts, with CC work 4 sts, with CC2 work 1 st, with MC work 9 sts, with CC2 work 2 sts, with CC work 3 sts, with CC2 work 2 sts, with MC work 8 sts, hdc in top of beg ch-2, turn.

Row 62: Ch 2, work 9 sts, with CC2 work 1 st, with CC work 4 sts, with CC2 work 2 sts, with MC work 8 sts, with CC2 work 2 sts, with CC work 4 sts, with CC2 work 1 st, with MC work 4 sts, with CC2 work 1 st, with CC work 3 sts, with CC2 work 1 st, with MC work 2 sts, with CC2 work 1 st, with CC work 3 sts, with CC2 work 1 st, with MC work 7 sts, with CC2 work 1 st, with CC work 2 sts, with CC2 work 1 st, with MC work 2 sts, hdc in top of beg ch-2, turn.

Row 63: Ch 2, work 2 sts, with CC2 work 1 st, with CC work 2 sts, with CC2 work 1 st, with MC work 7 sts, with CC2 work 1 st, with CC work 3 sts, with CC2 work 1 st, with MC work 2 sts, with CC2 work 1 st, with CC work 3 sts, with CC2 work 1 st, with MC work 3 sts, with CC2 work 2 sts, with CC work 4 sts, with CC2 work 1 st, with MC work 9 sts, with CC2 work 1 st, with CC work 4 sts, with CC2 work 2 sts, with MC work 9 sts, hdc in top of beg ch-2, turn.

Row 64: Ch 2, work 10 sts, with CC2 work 1 st, with CC work 4 sts, with CC2 work 2 sts, with MC work 8 sts, with CC2 work 2 sts, with CC work 3 sts, with CC2 work 2 sts, with MC work 3 sts, with CC2 work 1 st, with CC work 3 sts, with CC2 work 1 st, with MC work 2 sts, with CC2 work 1 st, with CC work 3 sts, with CC2 work 1 st, with MC work 7 sts, with CC2 work 1 st, with CC work 2 sts, with CC2 work 1 st, with MC work 2 sts, hdc in top of beg ch-2, turn.

Row 65: Ch 2, work 2 sts, with CC2 work 1 st, with CC work 2 sts, with CC2 work 1 st, with MC work 7 sts, with CC2 work 1 st, with CC work 3 sts, with CC2 work 1 st, with MC work 2 sts, with CC2 work 2 sts, with CC work 2 sts, with CC2 work 1 st, with MC work 3 sts, with CC2 work 1 st, with CC work 4 sts, with CC2 work 1 st, with MC work 9 sts, with CC2 work 1 st, with CC work 4 sts, with CC2 work 2 sts, with MC work 10 sts, hdc in top of beg ch-2, turn.

Row 66: Ch 2, work 11 sts, with CC2 work 2 sts, with CC work 3 sts, with CC2 work 2 sts, with MC work 8 sts, with CC2 work 1 st, with CC work 4 sts, with CC2 work 1 st, with MC work 3 sts, with CC2 work 1 st, with CC work 2 sts, with CC2 work 1 st, with MC work 3 sts, with CC2 work 1 st, with CC work 3 sts, with CC2 work 1 st, with MC work 7 sts, with CC2 work 1 st, with CC work 2 sts, with CC2 work 1 st, with MC work 2 sts, hdc in top of beg ch-2, turn.

Row 67: Ch 2, work 2 sts, with CC2 work 1 st, with CC work 2 sts, with CC2 work 2 sts, with MC work 6 sts, with CC2 work 2 sts, with CC work 2 sts, with CC2 work 2 sts, with MC work 2 sts, with CC2 work 1 st, with CC work 2 sts, with CC2 work 1 st, with MC work 3 sts, with CC2 work 1 st, with CC work 3 sts, with CC2 work 2 sts, with MC work 6 sts, with CC2 work 3 sts, with CC work 4 sts, with CC2 work 1 st, with MC work 12 sts, hdc in top of beg ch-2, turn.

Row 68: Ch 2, work 12 sts, with CC2 work 2 sts, with CC work 5 sts, with CC2 work 2 sts, with MC work 6 sts, with CC2 work 1 st, with CC work 3 sts, with CC2 work 2 sts, with MC work 2 sts, with CC2 work 1 st, with CC work 2 sts, with CC2 work 1 st, with MC work 2 sts, with CC2 work 1 st, with CC work 3 sts, with CC2 work 1 st, with MC work 7 sts, with CC2 work 1 st, with CC work 3 sts, with CC2 work 1 st, with MC work 2 sts, hdc in top of beg ch-2, turn.

Row 69: Ch 2, work 2 sts, with CC2 work 1 st, with CC work 3 sts, with CC2 work 2 sts, with MC work 6 sts, with CC2 work 1 st, with CC work 3 sts, with CC2 work 1 st, with MC work 2 sts, with CC2 work 1 st, with CC work 2 sts, with CC2 work 1 st, with MC work 2 sts, with CC2 work 1 st, with CC work 4 sts, with CC2 work 1 st, with MC work 5 sts, with CC2 work 2 sts, with CC work 5 sts, with CC2 work 1 st, with MC work 14 sts, hdc in top of beg ch-2, turn.

Row 70: Ch 2, work 14 sts, with CC2 work 2 sts, with CC work 5 sts, with CC2 work 2 sts, with MC work 4 sts, with CC2 work 1 st, with CC work 4 sts, with CC2 work 1 st, with MC work 2 sts, with CC2 work 1 st, with CC work 2 sts, with CC2 work 1 st, with MC work 2 sts, with CC2 work 1 st, with CC work 3 sts, with CC2 work 1 st, with MC work 5 sts, with CC2 work 2 sts, with CC work 3 sts, with CC2 work 2 sts, with MC work 2 sts, hdc in top of beg ch-2, turn.

Row 71: Ch 2, work 3 sts, with CC2 work 1 st, with CC work 4 sts, with CC2 work 1 st, with MC work 5 sts, with CC2 work 1 st, with CC work 3 sts, with CC2 work 1 st, with MC work 2 sts, with CC2 work 1 st, with CC work 2 sts, with CC2 work 2 sts, with MC work 1 st, with CC2 work 1 st, with CC work 4 sts, with CC2 work 1 st, with MC work 3 sts, with CC2 work 2 sts, with CC work 5 sts, with CC2 work 2 sts, with MC work 6 sts, with CC2 work 3 sts, with MC work 6 sts, hdc in top of beg ch-2, turn.

Row 72: Ch 2, work 5 sts, with CC2 work 2 sts, with CC work 1 st, with CC2 work 2 sts, with MC work 6 sts, with CC2 work 2 sts, with CC work 5 sts, with CC2 work 1 st, with MC work 3 sts, with CC2 work 2 sts, with CC work 3 sts, with CC2 work 1 st, with MC work 1 st, with CC2 work 1 st, with CC work 2 sts, with CC2 work 2 sts, with MC work 2 sts, with CC2 work 1 st, with CC work 3 sts, with CC2 work 1 st, with MC work 5 sts, with CC2 work 1 st, with CC work 3 sts, with CC2 work 2 sts, with MC work 3 sts, hdc in top of beg ch-2, turn.

Row 73: Ch 2, work 4 sts, with CC2 work 1 st, with CC work 3 sts, with CC2 work 1 st, with MC work 5 sts, with CC2 work 1 st, with CC work 3 sts, with CC2 work 1 st, with MC work 3 sts, with CC2 work 1 st, with CC work 2 sts, with CC2 work 1 st, with MC work 1 st, with CC2 work 1 st, with CC work 3 sts, with CC2 work 1 st, with MC work 3 sts, with CC2 work 2 sts, with CC work 4 sts, with CC2 work 2 sts, with MC work 7 sts, with CC2 work 1 st, with CC work 3 sts, with CC2 work 3 sts, with MC work 3 sts, hdc in top of beg ch-2, turn.

Row 74: Ch 2, work 3 sts, with CC2 work 1 st, with CC work 6 sts, with CC2 work 1 st, with MC work 7 sts, with CC2 work 1 st, with CC work 4 sts, with CC2 work 2 sts, with MC work 3 sts, with CC2 work 1 st, with CC work 3 sts, with CC2 work 1 st, with MC work 1 st, with CC2 work 1 st, with CC work 2 sts, with CC2 work 1 st, with MC work 3 sts, with CC2 work 1 st, with CC work 3 sts, with CC2 work 1 st, with MC work 5 sts, with CC2 work 1 st, with CC work 2 sts, with CC2 work 2 sts, with MC work 4 sts, hdc in top of beg ch-2, turn.

Row 75: Ch 2, work 5 sts, with CC2 work 1 st, with CC work 2 sts, with CC2 work 2 sts, with MC work 4 sts, with CC2 work 1 st, with CC work 3 sts, with CC2 work 2 sts, with MC work 2 sts, with CC2 work 1 st, with CC work 2 sts, with CC2 work 1 st, with MC work 1 st, with CC2 work 1 st, with CC work 3 sts, with CC2 work 1 st, with MC work 3 sts, with CC2 work 1 st, with CC work 4 sts, with CC2 work 2 sts, with MC work 7 sts, with CC2 work 1 st, with CC work 6 sts, with CC2 work 2 sts, with MC work 2 sts, hdc in top of beg ch-2, turn.

Row 76: Ch 2, work 2 sts, with CC2 work 1 st, with CC work 2 sts, with CC2 work 4 sts, with CC work 1 st, with CC2 work 1 st, with MC work 8 sts, with CC2 work 2 sts, with CC work 3 sts, with CC2 work 2 sts, with MC work 2 sts, with CC2 work 1 st, with CC work 3 sts, with CC2 work 1 st, with MC work 1 st, with CC2 work 1 st, with CC work 1 st, with CC2 work 2 sts, with MC work 2 sts, with CC2 work 1 st, with CC work 3 sts, with CC2 work 1 st, with MC work 5 sts, with CC2 work 1 st, with CC work 3 sts, with CC2 work 1 st, with MC work 5 sts, hdc in top of beg ch-2, turn.

Row 77: Ch 2, work 5 sts, with CC2 work 1 st, with CC work 3 sts, with CC2 work 1 st, with MC work 5 sts, with CC2 work 2 sts, with CC work 2 sts, with CC2 work 2 sts, with MC work 2 sts, with CC2 work 1 st, with CC work 1 st, with CC2 work 1 st, with MC work 1 st, with CC2 work 1 st, with CC work 3 sts, with CC2 work 1 st, with MC work 2 sts, with CC2 work 1 st, with CC work 4 sts, with CC2 work 1 st, with MC work 9 sts, with CC2 work 1 st, with CC work 1 st, with CC2 work 1 st, with MC work 2 sts, with CC2 work 1 st, with CC work 2 sts, with CC2 work 1 st, with MC work 2 sts, hdc in top of beg ch-2, turn.

Row 78: Ch 2, work 2 sts, with CC2 work 1 st, with CC work 2 sts, with CC2 work 1 st, with MC work 2 sts, with CC2 work 1 st, with CC work 1 st, with CC2 work 1 st, with MC work 10 sts, with CC2 work 1 st, with CC work 3 sts, with CC2 work 1 st, with MC work 2 sts, with CC2 work 1 st, with CC work 3 sts, with CC2 work 3 sts, with CC work 1 st, with CC2 work 1 st, with MC work 2 sts, with CC2 work 1 st, with CC work 3 sts, with CC2 work 1 st, with MC work 5 sts, with CC2 work 2 sts, with CC work 2 sts, with CC2 work 2 sts, with MC work 5 sts, hdc in top of beg ch-2, turn.

Row 79: Ch 2, work 5 sts, with CC2 work 2 sts, with CC work 3 sts, with CC2 work 1 st, with MC work 5 sts, with CC2 work 1 st, with CC work 3 sts, with CC2 work 2 sts, with MC work 1 st, with CC2 work 1 st, with CC work 2 sts, with CC2 work 2 sts, with CC work 3 sts, with CC2 work 1 st, with MC work 1 st, with CC2 work 1 st, with CC work 3 sts, with CC2 work 2 sts, with MC work 10 sts, with CC2 work 1 st, with CC work 1 st, with CC2 work 1 st, with MC work 2 sts, with CC2 work 2 sts, with CC work 1 st, with CC2 work 1 st, with MC work 2 sts, hdc in top of beg ch-2, turn.

Row 80: Ch 2, work 2 sts, with CC2 work 1 st, with CC work 1 st, with CC2 work 1 st, with MC work 2 sts, with CC2 work 1 st, with CC work 2 sts, with CC2 work 1 st, with MC work 3 sts, with CC2 work 6 sts, with MC work 2 sts, with CC2 work 1 st, with CC work 3 sts, with CC2 work 1 st, with MC work 1 st, with CC2 work 1 st, with CC work 3 sts, with CC2 work 2 sts, with CC work 1 st, with CC2 work 2 sts, with MC work 1 st, with CC2 work 1 st, with CC work 3 sts, with CC2 work 1 st, with MC work 6 sts, with CC2 work 1 st, with CC work 3 sts, with CC2 work 1 st, with MC work 6 sts, hdc in top of beg ch-2, turn.

Row 81: Ch 2, work 6 sts, with CC2 work 1 st, with CC work 3 sts, with CC2 work 2 sts, with MC work 5 sts, with CC2 work 2 sts, with CC work 2 sts, with CC2 work 1 st, with MC work 2 sts, with CC2 work 1 st, with CC work 2 sts, with CC2 work 1 st, with CC work 3 sts, with CC2 work 3 sts, with CC work 2 sts, with CC2 work 2 sts, with MC work 1 st, with CC2 work 2 sts, with CC work 5 sts, with CC2 work 2 sts, with MC work 2 sts, with CC2 work 1 st, with CC work 2 sts, with CC2 work 1 st, with MC work 1 st, with CC2 work 1 st, with CC work 1 st, with CC2 work 1 st, with MC work 2 sts, hdc in top of beg ch-2, turn.

Row 82: Ch 2, work 2 sts, with CC2 work 1 st, with CC work 1 st, with CC2 work 1 st, with MC work 2 sts, with CC2 work 2 sts, with MC work 3 sts, with CC2 work 1 st, with CC work 7 sts, with CC2 work 1 st, with MC work 2 sts, with CC2 work 1 st, with CC work 3 sts, with CC2 work 1 st, with CC work 7 sts, with CC2 work 1 st, with MC work 1 st, with CC2 work 1 st, with CC work 3 sts, with CC2 work 1 st, with MC work 6 sts, with CC2 work 1 st, with CC work 3 sts, with CC2 work 2 sts, with MC work 6 sts, hdc in top of beg ch-2, turn.

Row 83: Ch 2, work 7 sts, with CC2 work 1 st, with CC work 3 sts, with CC2 work 1 st, with MC work 6 sts, with CC2 work 1 st, with CC work 3 sts, with CC2 work 3 sts, with CC work 7 sts, with CC2 work 1 st, with CC work 3 sts, with CC2 work 3 sts, with CC work 8 sts, with CC2 work 2 sts, with MC work 5 sts, with CC2 work 1 st, with CC work 2 sts, with CC2 work 1 st, with MC work 2 sts, hdc in top of beg ch-2, turn.

Row 84: Ch 2, work 2 sts, with CC2 work 1 st, with CC work 3 sts, with CC2 work 1 st, with MC work 3 sts, with CC2 work 2 sts, with CC work 10 sts, with CC2 work 2 sts, with CC work 16 sts, with CC2 work 2 sts, with MC work 5 sts, with CC2 work 2 sts, with CC work 3 sts, with CC2 work 1 st, with MC work 7 sts, hdc in top of beg ch-2, turn.

Row 85: Ch 2, work 7 sts, with CC2 work 2 sts, with CC work 3 sts, with CC2 work 1 st, with MC work 6 sts, with CC2 work 2 sts, with CC work 14 sts, with CC2 work 2 sts, with CC work 4 sts, with CC2 work 6 sts, with CC work 3 sts, with CC2 work 1 st, with MC work

2 sts, with CC2 work 1 st, with CC work 2 sts, with CC2 work 2 sts, with MC work 2 sts, hdc in top of beg ch-2, turn.

Row 86: Ch 2, work 3 sts, with CC2 work 1 st, with CC work 3 sts, with CC2 work 3 sts, with CC work 2 sts, with CC2 work 2 sts, with MC work 4 sts, with CC2 work 3 sts, with CC work 2 sts, with CC2 work 2 sts, with CC work 14 sts, with CC2 work 1 st, with MC work 6 sts, with CC2 work 2 sts, with CC work 2 sts, with CC2 work 2 sts, with MC work 8 sts, hdc in top of beg ch-2, turn.

Row 87: Ch 2, work 9 sts, with CC2 work 1 st, with CC work 3 sts, with CC2 work 1 st, with MC work 6 sts, with CC2 work 1 st, with CC work 18 sts, with CC2 work 1 st, with MC work 7 sts, with CC2 work 2 sts, with CC work 6 sts, with CC2 work 2 sts, with MC work 3 sts, hdc in top of beg ch-2, turn.

Row 88: Ch 2, work 4 sts, with CC2 work 1 st, with CC work 5 sts, with CC2 work 2 sts, with MC work 8 sts, with CC2 work 2 sts, with CC work 17 sts, with CC2 work 1 st, with MC work 3 sts, with CC2 work 3 sts, with CC work 4 sts, with CC2 work 1 st, with MC work 9 sts, hdc in top of beg ch-2, turn.

Row 89: Ch 2, work 9 sts, with CC2 work 2 sts, with CC work 5 sts, with CC2 work 5 sts, with CC work 17 sts, with CC2 work 1 st, with MC work 10 sts, with CC2 work 1 st, with CC work 4 sts, with CC2 work 2 sts, with MC work 4 sts, hdc in top of beg ch-2, turn.

Row 90: Ch 2, work 5 sts, with CC2 work 2 sts, with CC work 2 sts, with CC2 work 1 st, with MC work 6 sts, with CC2 work 7 sts, with CC work 17 sts, with CC2 work 2 sts, with CC work 6 sts, with CC2 work 2 sts, with MC work 10 sts, hdc in top of beg ch-2, turn.

Row 91: Ch 2, work 11 sts, with CC2 work 2 sts, with CC work 24 sts, with CC2 work 2 sts, with CC work 4 sts, with CC2 work 2 sts, with MC work 5 sts, with CC2 work 4 sts, with MC work 6 sts, hdc in top of beg ch-2, turn.

Row 92: Ch 2, work 15 sts, with CC2 work 1 st, with CC work 29 sts, with CC2 work 3 sts, with MC work 12 sts, hdc in top of beg ch-2, turn.

Row 93: Ch 2, work 14 sts, with CC2 work 2 sts, with CC work 28 sts, with CC2 work 3 sts, with MC work 13 sts, hdc in top of beg ch-2, turn.

Row 94: Ch 2, work 13 sts, with CC2 work 1 st, with CC work 26 sts, with CC2 work 5 sts, with MC work 15 sts, hdc in top of beg ch-2, turn.

Row 95: Ch 2, work 19 sts, with CC2 work 2 sts, with CC work 16 sts, with CC2 work 2 sts, with CC work 7 sts, with CC2 work 2 sts, with MC work 12 sts, hdc in top of beg ch-2, turn

Row 96: Ch 2, work 12 sts, with CC2 work 1 st, with CC work 5 sts, with CC2 work 6 sts, with CC work 16 sts, with CC2 work 1 st, with MC work 19 sts, hdc in top of beg ch-2, turn.

Row 97: Ch 2, work 18 sts, with CC2 work 2 sts, with CC work 16 sts, with CC2 work 1 st, with MC work 4 sts, with CC2 work 2 sts, with CC work 4 sts, with CC2 work 1 st, with MC work 12 sts, hdc in top of beg ch-2, turn.

Row 98: Ch 2, work 11 sts, with CC2 work 2 sts, with CC work 3 sts, with CC2 work 2 sts, with MC work 5 sts, with CC2 work 1 st, with CC work 14 sts, with CC2 work 1 st, with CC work 2 sts, with CC2 work 3 sts, with MC work 16 sts, hdc in top of beg ch-2, turn.

Row 99: Ch 2, work 14 sts, with CC2 work 4 sts, with CC work 2 sts, with CC2 work 2 sts, with CC work 14 sts, with CC2 work 2 sts, with MC work 5 sts, with CC2 work 2 sts, with CC work 3 sts, with CC2 work 1 st, with MC work 11 sts, hdc in top of beg ch-2, turn

Row 100: Ch 2, work 11 sts, with CC2 work 1 st, with CC work 3 sts, with CC2 work 1 st, with MC work 6 sts, with CC2 work 1 st, with CC work 16 sts, with CC2 work 1 st, with CC work 4 sts, with CC2 work 4 sts, with MC work 12 sts, hdc in top of beg ch-2, turn.

Row 101: Ch 2, work 10 sts, with CC2 work 3 sts, with CC work 5 sts, with CC2 work 3 sts, with CC work 16 sts, with CC2 work 1 st, with MC work 6 sts, with CC2 work 1 st, with CC work 3 sts, with CC2 work 1 st, with MC work 11 sts, hdc in top of beg ch-2, turn

Row 102: Ch 2, work 10 sts, with CC2 work 2 sts, with CC work 2 sts, with CC2 work 2 sts, with MC work 5 sts, with CC2 work 2 sts, with CC work 16 sts, with CC2 work 1 st, with MC work 2 sts, with CC2 work 2 sts, with CC work 5 sts, with CC2 work 2 sts, with MC work 9 sts, hdc in top of beg ch-2, turn.

Row 103: Ch 2, work 8 sts, with CC2 work 2 sts, with CC work 5 sts, with CC2 work 2 sts, with MC work 3 sts, with CC2 work 1 st, with CC work 17 sts, with CC2 work 1 st, with MC work 6 sts, with CC2 work 1 st, with CC work 3 sts, with CC2 work 1 st, with MC work 10 sts, hdc in top of beg ch-2, turn.

Row 104: Ch 2, work 10 sts, with CC2 work 1 st, with CC work 3 sts, with CC2 work 1 st, with MC work 5 sts, with CC2 work 2 sts, with CC work 17 sts, with CC2 work 2 sts, with MC work 3 sts, with CC2 work 3 sts, with CC work 4 sts, with CC2 work 2 sts, with MC work 7 sts, hdc in top of beg ch-2, turn.

Row 105: Ch 2, work 6 sts, with CC2 work 2 sts, with CC work 4 sts, with CC2 work 2 sts, with MC work 5 sts, with CC2 work 1 st, with CC work 19 sts, with CC2 work 1 st, with MC work 5 sts, with CC2 work 1 st, with CC work 3 sts, with CC2 work 1 st, with MC work 10 sts, hdc in top of beg ch-2, turn.

Row 106: Ch 2, work 10 sts, with CC2 work 1 st, with CC work 2 sts, with CC2 work 1 st, with MC work 6 sts, with CC2 work 1 st, with CC work 19 sts, with CC2 work 1 st, with MC work 6 sts, with CC2 work 1 st, with CC work 5 sts, with CC2 work 1 st, with MC work 6 sts, hdc in top of beg ch-2, turn.

Row 107: Ch 2, work 5 sts, with CC2 work 2 sts, with CC work 4 sts, with CC2 work 2 sts, with MC work 5 sts, with CC2 work 2 sts, with CC work 19 sts, with CC2 work 2 sts, with MC work 5 sts, with CC2 work 1 st, with CC work 2 sts, with CC2 work 1 st, with MC work 10 sts, hdc in top of beg ch-2, turn.

Row 108: Ch 2, work 10 sts, with CC2 work 1 st, with CC work 2 sts, with CC2 work 1 st, with MC work 5 sts, with CC2 work 1 st, with CC work 21 sts, with CC2 work 1 st, with MC work 6 sts, with CC2 work 2 sts, with CC work 4 sts, with CC2 work 1 st, with MC work 5 sts, hdc in top of beg ch-2, turn.

Row 109: Ch 2, work 4 sts, with CC2 work 2 sts, with CC work 3 sts, with CC2 work 2 sts, with MC work 7 sts, with CC2 work 1 st, with CC work 21 sts, with CC2 work 1 st, with MC work 5 sts, with CC2 work 1 st, with CC work 2 sts, with CC2 work 1 st, with MC work 10 sts, hdc in top of beg ch-2, turn.

Row 110: Ch 2, work 10 sts, with CC2 work 1 st, with CC work 2 sts, with CC2 work 1 st, with MC work 5 sts, with CC2 work 1 st, with CC work 22 sts, with CC2 work 1 st, with MC work 7 sts, with CC2 work 2 sts, with CC work 3 sts, with CC2 work 1 st, with MC work 4 sts, hdc in top of beg ch-2, turn.

Row 111: Ch 2, work 4 sts, with CC2 work 1 st, with CC work 2 sts, with CC2 work 2 sts, with MC work 7 sts, with CC2 work 2 sts, with CC work 22 sts, with CC2 work 2 sts, with MC work 4 sts, with CC2 work 1 st, with CC work 2 sts, with CC2 work 1 st, with MC work 10 sts, hdc in top of beg ch-2, turn.

Row 112: Ch 2, work 10 sts, with CC2 work 1 st, with CC work 2 sts, with CC2 work 1 st, with MC work 4 sts, with CC2 work 1 st, with CC work 24 sts, with CC2 work 1 st, with MC work 8 sts, with CC2 work 1 st, with CC work 2 sts, with CC2 work 2 sts, with MC work 3 sts, hdc in top of beg ch-2, turn.

Row 113: Ch 2, work 3 sts, with CC2 work 1 st, with CC work 2 sts, with CC2 work 2 sts, with MC work 8 sts, with CC2 work 1 st, with CC work 24 sts, with CC2 work 1 st, with MC work 4 sts, with CC2 work 1 st, with CC work 2 sts, with CC2 work 1 st, with MC work 10 sts, hdc in top of beg ch-2, turn.

Row 114: Ch 2, work 10 sts, with CC2 work 1 st, with CC work 2 sts, with CC2 work 1 st, with MC work 4 sts, with CC2 work 1 st, with CC work 24 sts, with CC2 work 2 sts, with MC work 8 sts, with CC2 work 1 st, with CC work 2 sts, with CC2 work 1 st, with MC work 3 sts, hdc in top of beg ch-2, turn.

Row 115: Ch 2, work 3 sts, with CC2 work 1 st, with CC work 2 sts, with CC2 work 1 st, with MC work 8 sts, with CC2 work 1 st, with CC work 25 sts, with CC2 work 1 st, with MC work 4 sts, with CC2 work 1 st, with CC work 2 sts, with CC2 work 2 sts, with MC work 9 sts, hdc in top of beg ch-2, turn.

Row 116: Ch 2, work 9 sts, with CC2 work 1 st, with CC work 3 sts, with CC2 work 1 st, with MC work 3 sts, with CC2 work 2 sts, with CC work 25 sts, with CC2 work 1 st, with MC work 8 sts, with CC2 work 1 st, with CC work 2 sts, with CC2 work 1 st, with MC work 3 sts, hdc in top of beg ch-2, turn.

Row 117: Ch 2, work 3 sts, with CC2 work 1 st, with CC work 2 sts, with CC2 work 1 st, with MC work 8 sts, with CC2 work 1 st, with CC work 26 sts, with CC2 work 1 st, with MC work 3 sts, with CC2 work 2 sts, with CC work 2 sts, with CC2 work 2 sts, with MC work 3 sts, with CC2 work 3 sts, with MC work 2 sts, hdc in top of beg ch-2, turn.

Row 118: Ch 2, work 2 sts, with CC2 work 1 st, with CC work 1 st, with CC2 work 2 sts, with MC work 2 sts, with CC2 work 1 st, with CC work 3 sts, with CC2 work 1 st, with MC work 4 sts, with CC2 work 1 st, with CC work 26 sts, with CC2 work 1 st, with MC work 8 sts, with CC2 work 1 st, with CC work 2 sts, with CC2 work 1 st, with MC work 3 sts, hdc in top of beg ch-2, turn.

Row 119: Ch 2, work 3 sts, with CC2 work 1 st, with CC work 2 sts, with CC2 work 2 sts, with MC work 7 sts, with CC2 work 1 st, with CC work 26 sts, with CC2 work 1 st, with MC work 4 sts, with CC2 work 1 st, with CC work 3 sts, with CC2 work 4 sts, with CC work 2 sts, with CC2 work 1 st, with MC work 2 sts, hdc in top of beg ch-2, turn.

Row 120: Ch 2, work 3 sts, with CC2 work 1 st, with CC work 7 sts, with CC2 work 2 sts, with MC work 4 sts, with CC2 work 1 st, with CC work 25 sts, with CC2 work 2 sts, with MC work 2 sts, with CC2 work 3 sts, with MC work 2 sts, with CC2 work 1 st, with CC work 3 sts, with CC2 work 1 st, with MC work 3 sts, hdc in top of beg ch-2, turn.

Row 121: Ch 2, work 3 sts, with CC2 work 1 st, with CC work 3 sts, with CC2 work 4 sts, with CC work 1 st, with CC2 work 2 sts, with MC work 2 sts, with CC2 work 1 st, with CC work 25 sts, with CC2 work 1 st, with MC work 5 sts, with CC2 work 2 sts, with CC work 5 sts, with CC2 work 2 sts, with MC work 3 sts, hdc in top of beg ch-2, turn.

Row 122: Ch 2, work 4 sts, with CC2 work 2 sts, with CC work 2 sts, with CC2 work 3 sts, with MC work 6 sts, with CC2 work 1 st, with CC work 25 sts, with CC2 work 1 st, with MC work 2 sts, with CC2 work 1 st, with CC work 3 sts, with CC2 work 2 sts, with CC work 3 sts, with CC2 work 2 sts, with MC work 3 sts, hdc in top of beg ch-2, turn.

Row 123: Ch 2, work 4 sts, with CC2 work 2 sts, with CC work 7 sts, with CC2 work 1 st, with MC work 2 sts, with CC2 work 2 sts, with CC work 23 sts, with CC2 work 2 sts, with MC work 8 sts, with CC2 work 4 sts, with MC work 5 sts, hdc in top of beg ch-2, turn.

Row 124: Ch 2, work 18 sts, with CC2 work 1 st, with CC work 23 sts, with CC2 work 1 st, with MC work 3 sts, with CC2 work 1 st, with CC work 6 sts, with CC2 work 2 sts, with MC work 5 sts, hdc in top of beg ch-2, turn.

Row 125: Ch 2, work 6 sts, with CC2 work 2 sts, with CC work 4 sts, with CC2 work 2 sts, with MC work 3 sts, with CC2 work 1 st, with CC work 23 sts, with CC2 work 1 st, with MC work 18 sts, hdc in top of beg ch-2.

Fasten off all colors.

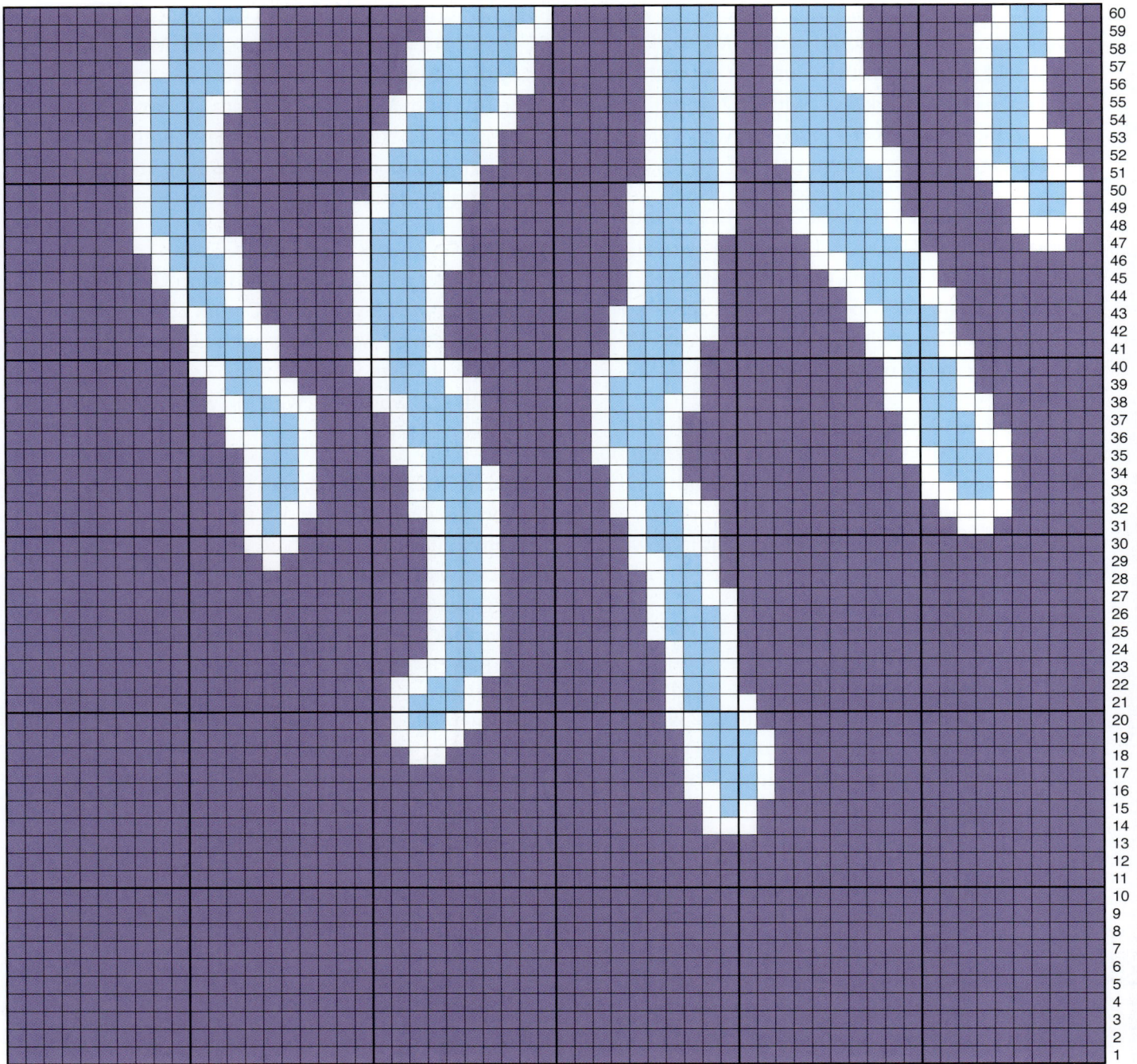

You Octopi My Heart
Chart (A)

COLOR KEY
- ☐ Contrasting Color - Silhouette
- ☐ Contrasting Color 2 - Outline
- ☐ Main Color - Background

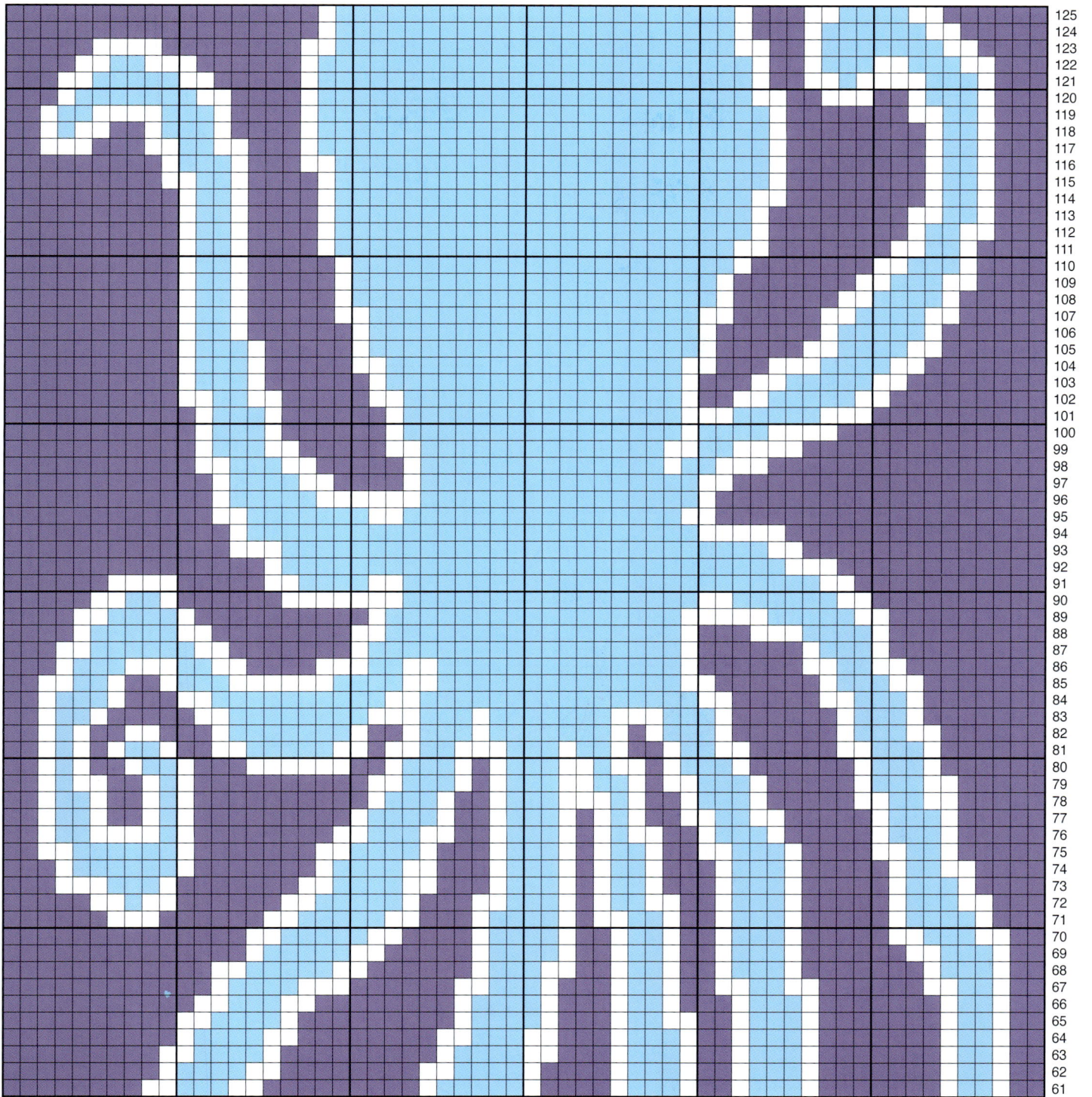

You Octopi My Heart
Chart (B)

Edging

Note: Blanket is reversible up to this point. Decide which side you like as the front and make sure right side is facing you as you work the Edging and Border.

Rnd 1 (RS): Hold blanket with foundation ch at top, join CC2 in first ch in right-hand corner, ch 1, 3 sc in first ch, sc in each ch across to last ch, 3 sc in last ch, rotate blanket to work in row ends, work 3 sc for every 2 rows across side, rotate blanket to work across top row, 3 sc in first st, sc in each st across to last st, 3 sc in last st, rotate blanket to work in row ends, work 3 sc for every 2 rows across side, join in top of first sc. Fasten off. *(126 sts along top and bottom, 188 sts along each side; 628 sts around blanket)*

Twisting Border

Work same as Twisting Border on page 5. ●

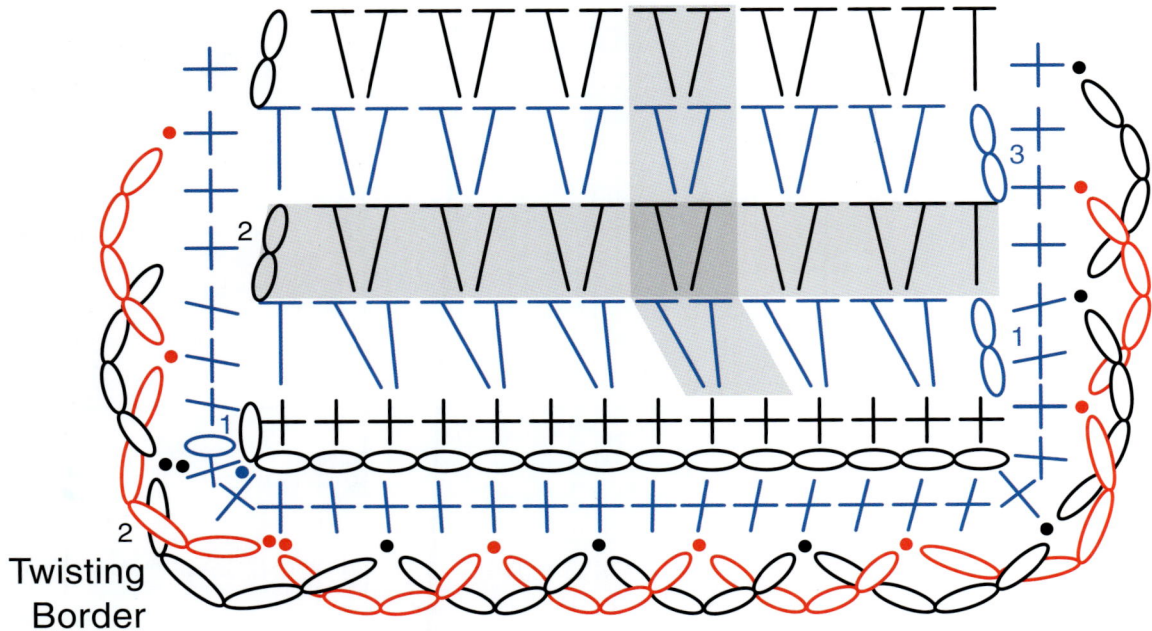

You Octopi My Heart
Reduced Sample of Stitch Diagram
Note: Rep shown in gray.

STITCH KEY	
⬯	Chain (ch)
•	Slip stitch (sl st)
+	Single crochet (sc)
T	Half double crochet (hdc)
V	Mini V-stitch (mini V-st)

STITCH GUIDE

STITCH ABBREVIATIONS

beg . . . . begin/begins/beginning
bpdc . . . . back post double crochet
bpsc . . . . .back post single crochet
bptr . . . . .back post treble crochet
CC . . . . contrasting color
ch(s) . . . . .chain(s)
ch- . . . . .refers to chain or space
  previously made (i.e., ch-1 space)
ch sp(s) . . . . chain space(s)
cl(s) . . . . cluster(s)
cm . . . . centimeter(s)
dc . . . . double crochet (singular/plural)
dc dec . . . . double crochet 2 or more
  stitches together, as indicated
dec . . . . decrease/decreases/decreasing
dtr . . . . double treble crochet
ext . . . . .extended
fpdc . . . . front post double crochet
fpsc . . . . front post single crochet
fptr . . . . front post treble crochet
g . . . . .gram(s)
hdc . . . . half double crochet
hdc dec . . . . half double crochet 2 or more
  stitches together, as indicated
inc . . . . increase/increases/increasing
lp(s) . . . . .loop(s)
MC . . . . .main color
mm . . . . millimeter(s)
oz . . . . ounce(s)
pc . . . . popcorn(s)
rem . . . . .remain/remains/remaining
rep(s) . . . . repeat(s)
rnd(s) . . . . .round(s)
RS . . . . .right side
sc . . . . single crochet (singular/plural)
sc dec . . . . .single crochet 2 or more
  stitches together, as indicated
sk . . . . .skip/skipped/skipping
sl st(s) . . . . slip stitch(es)
sp(s) . . . . space(s)/spaced
st(s) . . . . stitch(es)
tog . . . . .together
tr . . . . treble crochet
trtr . . . . .triple treble
WS . . . . wrong side
yd(s) . . . . .yard(s)
yo . . . . yarn over

YARN CONVERSION

OUNCES TO GRAMS		GRAMS TO OUNCES	
1	28.4	25	7/8
2	56.7	40	1 2/3
3	85.0	50	1 3/4
4	113.4	100	3 1/2

UNITED STATES		UNITED KINGDOM
sl st (slip stitch)	=	sc (single crochet)
sc (single crochet)	=	dc (double crochet)
hdc (half double crochet)	=	htr (half treble crochet)
dc (double crochet)	=	tr (treble crochet)
tr (treble crochet)	=	dtr (double treble crochet)
dtr (double treble crochet)	=	ttr (triple treble crochet)
skip	=	miss

Reverse single crochet (reverse sc): Ch 1, sk first st, working from left to right, insert hook in next st from front to back, draw up lp on hook, yo and draw through both lps on hook.

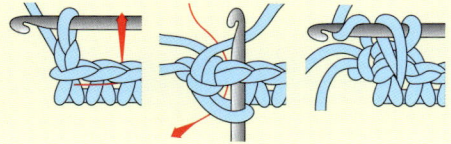

Chain (ch): Yo, pull through lp on hook.

Single crochet (sc): Insert hook in st, yo, pull through st, yo, pull through both lps on hook.

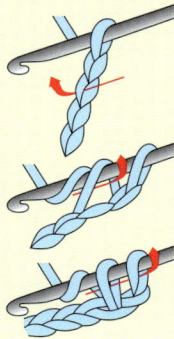

Double crochet (dc): Yo, insert hook in st, yo, pull through st, [yo, pull through 2 lps] twice.

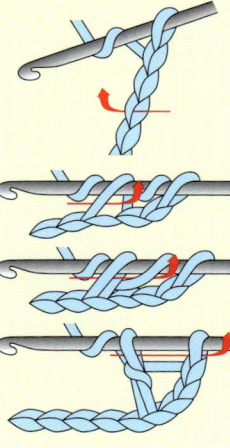

Front loop (front lp) Back loop (back lp)

Front Loop   Back Loop

Front post stitch (fp): Back post stitch (bp): When working post st, insert hook from right to left around post of st on previous row.

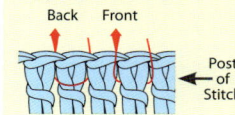

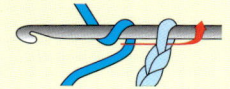

Back   Front

← Post of Stitch

Half double crochet (hdc): Yo, insert hook in st, yo, pull through st, yo, pull through all 3 lps on hook.

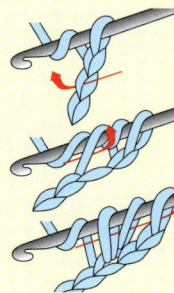

Double treble crochet (dtr): Yo 3 times, insert hook in st, yo, pull through st, [yo, pull through 2 lps] 4 times.

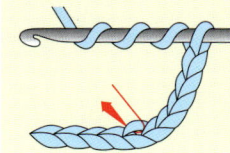

Slip stitch (sl st): Insert hook in st, pull through both lps on hook.

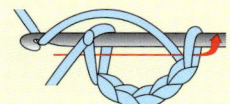

Chain color change (ch color change) Yo with new color, draw through last lp on hook.

Double crochet color change (dc color change) Drop first color, yo with new color, draw through last 2 lps of st.

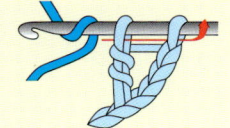

Treble crochet (tr): Yo twice, insert hook in st, yo, pull through st, [yo, pull through 2 lps] 3 times.

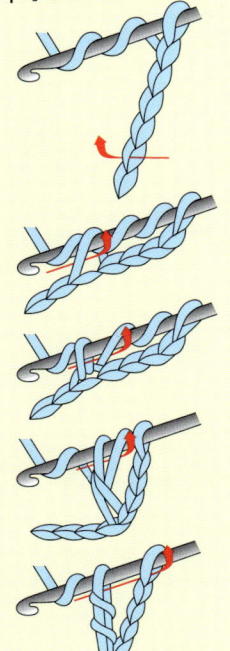

Single crochet decrease (sc dec): (Insert hook, yo, draw lp through) in each of the sts indicated, yo, draw through all lps on hook.

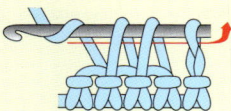

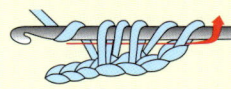

Example of 2-sc dec

Half double crochet decrease (hdc dec): (Yo, insert hook, yo, draw lp through) in each of the sts indicated, yo, draw through all lps on hook.

Example of 2-hdc dec

Double crochet decrease (dc dec): (Yo, insert hook, yo, draw lp through, yo, draw through 2 lps on hook) in each of the sts indicated, yo, draw through all lps on hook.

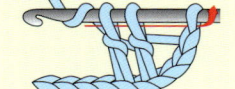

Example of 2-dc dec

Treble crochet decrease (tr dec): Holding back last lp of each st, tr in each of the sts indicated, yo, pull through all lps on hook.

Example of 2-tr dec

Metric Conversion Charts

METRIC CONVERSIONS

yards	x	.9144	=	metres (m)
yards	x	91.44	=	centimetres (cm)
inches	x	2.54	=	centimetres (cm)
inches	x	25.40	=	millimetres (mm)
inches	x	.0254	=	metres (m)

centimetres	x	.3937	=	inches
metres	x	1.0936	=	yards

INCHES INTO MILLIMETRES & CENTIMETRES (Rounded off slightly)

inches	mm	cm	inches	cm	inches	cm	inches	cm
1/8	3	0.3	5	12.5	21	53.5	38	96.5
1/4	6	0.6	5 1/2	14	22	56	39	99
3/8	10	1	6	15	23	58.5	40	101.5
1/2	13	1.3	7	18	24	61	41	104
5/8	15	1.5	8	20.5	25	63.5	42	106.5
3/4	20	2	9	23	26	66	43	109
7/8	22	2.2	10	25.5	27	68.5	44	112
1	25	2.5	11	28	28	71	45	114.5
1 1/4	32	3.2	12	30.5	29	73.5	46	117
1 1/2	38	3.8	13	33	30	76	47	119.5
1 3/4	45	4.5	14	35.5	31	79	48	122
2	50	5	15	38	32	81.5	49	124.5
2 1/2	65	6.5	16	40.5	33	84	50	127
3	75	7.5	17	43	34	86.5		
3 1/2	90	9	18	46	35	89		
4	100	10	19	48.5	36	91.5		
4 1/2	115	11.5	20	51	37	94		

KNITTING NEEDLES CONVERSION CHART

Canada/U.S.	0	1	2	3	4	5	6	7	8	9	10	10½	11	13	15
Metric (mm)	2	2¼	2¾	3¼	3½	3¾	4	4½	5	5½	6	6½	8	9	10

CROCHET HOOKS CONVERSION CHART

Canada/U.S.	1/B	2/C	3/D	4/E	5/F	6/G	8/H	9/I	10/J	10½/K	N
Metric (mm)	2.25	2.75	3.25	3.5	3.75	4.25	5	5.5	6	6.5	9.0

Annie's

Tails of the Sea: Children's Crochet Blankets is published by Annie's, 306 East Parr Road, Berne, IN 46711. Printed in USA. Copyright © 2018 Annie's. All rights reserved. This publication may not be reproduced in part or in whole without written permission from the publisher.

RETAIL STORES: If you would like to carry this publication or any other Annie's publication, visit AnniesWSL.com.

Every effort has been made to ensure that the instructions in this publication are complete and accurate. We cannot, however, take responsibility for human error, typographical mistakes or variations in individual work. Please visit AnniesCustomerService.com to check for pattern updates.

ISBN: 978-1-59012-880-0

1 2 3 4 5 6 7 8 9